English Connect

365+

English Connect

365+

Business

Eric Thompson

PARTRIDGE

To order additional copies of this book, contact
Toll Free 800 101 2657 (Singapore)
Toll Free 1 800 81 7340 (Malaysia)
orders.singapore@partridgepublishing.com

www.partridgepublishing.com/singapore

INTRODUCTION

I want to congratulate you for having this book in your possession. This is the third in the English connect 365+ series. I believe it will serve the purpose for which you have it and help you to connect.

The world seems like it is shrinking every day. Rapid globalization means that doing business with people from other countries and continents is more common than ever before. On one hand, learning another language is being a responsible global citizen. On the other hand, it gives us edges professionally when we understand and acquire the skill to be able to communicate professionally.

You may be wondering what the difference is, after all I can speak English well and I can read this, I have studied the first two English connect 365+series, what is the difference? What else do I need to learn? Just look at it as being the same as 'normal' English, just with different verbs and nouns.

In a nutshell, there's no big difference. For instance, Instead of saying Enough we say, Sufficient or instead of 'Can you send me the invoice please?' we say, 'Can you forward me the invoice, please?' Instead of, 'Let's talk about the staff bonus' we might say, 'Let's discuss the staff bonus policy'.

There are other few things you need to understand too;

1.   First, you need to understand the difference between formal and informal English.
2.   Second, you need to understand when either is appropriate to use.
3.   Finally, you need opportunities to practice both.

The last part is very crucial in retaining what you have learned. You need to learn actively by taking every opportunity that comes your way by practicing your English.

Take a look at the following cone of learning, it may look familiar:

After 2 weeks we tend to remember	Cone of Learning	Nature of Involvement
90% of what we say and do	Doing the Real Thing	Active
	Simulating the Real Experience	
	Doing a Dramatic Presentation	
70% of what we say	Giving a Talk	
	Participating in a Discussion	
50% of what we hear and see	Seeing it Done on Location	Passive
	Watching a Demonstration	
	Looking at an Exhibit Watching a Demonstration	
	Watching a Movie	
30% of what we see	Looking at Pictures	
20% of what we hear	Hearing Words	
10% of what we read	Reading	

Source: Cone of Learning adapted from Dale, (1969)

As you can see that the tendency to remember is higher when we are **active** learner than when we are **passive**. This picture confirms that practice makes perfection and that when one teaches two learn and also that it pays to share and be generous in many ways. The bottom line, study these terms used in business world and make sure you practice both formal and informal English constantly.

Try as much as possible to study at least one term or phrase a day, some may be familiar though, make or **cook** your own and see how you'll connect in both regular conversation situation and business world.

Happy English learning!

1. RED TAPE

Meaning:
Red tape is a business term that means a strict adherence to rules and regulations so that a procedure seems to take longer than necessary.

Example:
It takes a long time to set up a company in some countries because of all the red tape involved in getting government permits.

Now look it up to understand more, and then make your sentences.

1. _____.
2. _____.
3. _____.

2. MORAL STANDARDS

Meaning:
Moral standard is a code of practice which shows how a group of people or professionals behave or should interact with each other.

Examples:
1. Many people argue whether objective moral standards really exist.
2. Employees need a friendly and fair atmosphere, which is impossible when moral standards are corrupted in a company.

Now look it up to understand more, and then make your sentences.

1. _____.
2. _____.
3. _____.

3. Basic Aim

Meaning:
It is a specific goal or purpose you attempt or intend to reach.

Examples:
1. The basic aims of the government's new policy are to reduce the budget deficit and provide people with sufficient healthcare.
2. The basic aims of our business activity this month are to increase sales and get new customers.

Now look it up to understand more, and then make your sentences.

1. _____.
2. _____.
3. _____.

4. Production

Meaning:
The processes and methods used to transform tangible inputs (raw materials, semi-finished goods etc.) and intangible inputs (ideas, information, knowledge) into goods or services.

Example:
Having a good production team can help your business stay up to the task of handling all of your demands.

Now look it up to understand more, and then make your sentences.

1. _____.
2. _____.
3. _____.

5. PRODUCTION CAPACITY

Meaning:
Production capacity is the volume of products that can be generated by a production plant or enterprise in a given period by using current resources.

Examples:
1. Production capacity has decreased recently due to high prices of resources.
2. We've changed the staff in our factories and employed more professionals, which resulted in excellent production capacity.

Now look it up to understand more, and then make your sentences.

1. _____.
2. _____.
3. _____.

6. PRODUCT

Meaning:
A good, idea, method, information, object or service created as a result of a process and serves a need or satisfies a want.

Example:
He had great idea for a product, but he didn't have enough money to make or produce it on his own.

Now look it up to understand more, and then make your sentences.

1. _____.
2. _____.
3. _____.

7. Commodity

Meaning:
A reasonably interchangeable good or material bought and sold freely as an article of commerce. Commodities include agricultural products, fuels, and metals and are traded in bulk on a commodity exchange or spot market.

Example:
In Iowa, corn is a very hot commodity that is widely produced, especially when growing conditions are optimal, and is even exported to supply the food source in other countries.

Now look it up to understand more, and then make your sentences.

1. _____.
2. _____.
3. _____.

8. Emerging Markets

Meaning:
New market structures arising from digitalization, deregulation, globalization, and open-standards that are shifting the balance of economic power from the sellers to the buyers.

Example:
The situation of emerging markets is difficult at the time of the economic crisis.

Now look it up to understand more, and then make your sentences.

1. _____.
2. _____.
3. _____.

9. DISMISSAL

Meaning:
DISMISSAL is the termination of the contract of employment of an employee by his or her employer in a correct, fair, and lawful manner.

Examples:
1. She sued her employer for unfair dismissal. She was fired because she dyed her hair red.
2. Many people faced dismissals at the time the company had financial problems.

Now look it up to understand more, and then make your sentences.

1. _____.
2. _____.
3. _____.

10. MAKE REDUNDANT

Meaning:
To Make Redundant is the elimination of jobs or job categories caused by downsizing, rightsizing, or outsourcing.

Examples:
1. A lot of workers were made redundant to reduce the expenses of the company.
2. After his lies and frauds were uncovered, the boss made him redundant.

Now look it up to understand more, and then make your sentences.

1. _____.
2. _____.
3. _____.

11. BOARD OF DIRECTORS

Meaning:
It is the Governing body (called the board) of an incorporated firm. Its members (directors) are elected normally by the subscribers (stockholders) of the firm (generally at an annual general meeting or AGM) to govern the firm and look after the subscribers' interests.

Examples:
1. The company's success depends a lot on the board of directors and their leadership skills.
2. The appointment of the new board of directors resulted in a huge disorder in our company.

Now look it up to understand more, and then make your sentences.

1. _____.
2. _____.
3. _____.

12. VELOCITY OF MONEY

Meaning:
Velocity of money or velocity of circulation is the rate at which money circulates, changes hands, or turns over in an economy in a given period.

Example:
The velocity of money greatly increases in times of economy prosperity and at holiday season, especially from Thanksgiving through New Year's Day.

Now look it up to understand more, and then make your sentences.

1. _____.
2. _____.
3. _____.

13. REVENUE

Meaning:
The income generated from sale of goods or services, or any other use of capital or assets, associated with the main operations of an organization before any costs or expenses are deducted.

Example:
The company last year made a substantial amount of revenue, consequence of increased sales, putting it at the top of the 'Most Successful' list of businesses.

Now look it up to understand more, and then make your sentences.

1. _____.
2. _____.
3. _____.

14. ESTIMATE

Meaning:
Approximation, prediction, or projection of a quantity based on experience and/or information available at the time, with the recognition that other pertinent facts are unclear or unknown.

Example:
Damage from the hurricane is estimated (to be) in the billions of dollars.

Now look it up to understand more, and then make your sentences.

1. _____.
2. _____.
3. _____.

15. Consumer

Meaning:
A Consumer is a person or an organization that uses a commodity or service.

Example:
Many consumers are still not comfortable making purchases on the Internet.

Now look it up to understand more, and then make your sentences.

1. _____.

2. _____.

3. _____.

Treasure Box 1

Downsizing: When a company downsizes, it is attempting to find ways to improve efficiency and increase profitability.
Rightsizing is the act or process of reducing the workforce at a company to the perceived correct number.
Outsourcing is a practice used by different companies to reduce costs by transferring portions of work to outside suppliers rather than completing it internally.

16. ECONOMY

Meaning:
Economy is an entire network of producers, distributors, and consumers of goods and services in a local, regional, or national community.

Example:
In 2008, the economy took a real down turn, causing the loss of jobs and money everywhere, and has yet to reach the point in where it was before.

Now look it up to understand more, and then make your sentences.

1. _____.
2. _____.
3. _____.

17. DEMAND

Meaning:
Demand is the total amount of funds which individuals or organizations want to commit for spending on goods or services over a specific period.

Example:
The company increased its production of the new sneaker after a recent advertising campaign made the demand for the product soar.

Now look it up to understand more, and then make your sentences.

1. _____.
2. _____.
3. _____.

18. SUPPLY

Meaning:
The total amount of a product (good or service) available for purchase at any specified price.

Example:
When you put out a new product and everyone likes it you must increase your supply to handle the demand.

Now look it up to understand more, and then make your sentences.

1. _____.
2. _____.
3. _____.

19. EQUILIBRIUM

Meaning:
A market is said to be in equilibrium if the amount of goods that buyers wish to buy at the current price is matched by the amount the sellers want to sell at that price.

Example:
The company wanted to price the new product where they would reach equilibrium. They wanted to play the volume game, so they priced it so demand would equal supply

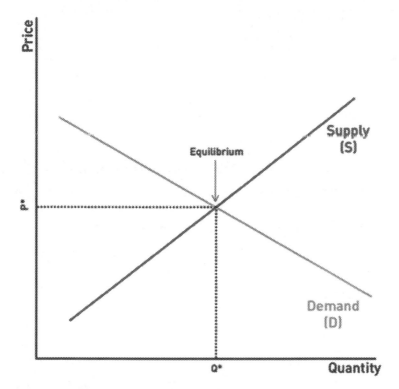

In the diagram above, supply(S) and demand(D) illustrated at a price of (P) and a quantity of (Q), the quantity demanded and the supply demanded intersect at the **Equilibrium** Price.

Now look it up to understand more, and then make your sentences.

1. _____.
2. _____.
3. _____.

20. Product liability

Meaning:
General liability or obligation of a producer (or supplier) of a good or service to make restitution for loss associated with its use, such as personal injury or property damage.

Example:
The car dealer was obliged by product liability to recall 50 new cars he had sold because they were defective.

Now look it up to understand more, and then make your sentences.

1. _____.
2. _____.
3. _____.

REVIEW QUIZ

Match the terms in the box with their appropriate meanings.

> 1. red tape, 2. moral standards, 3. basic aim, 4. Production,
> 5. production capacity 6. Product, 7. Commodity,
> 8. Emerging Markets, 9. Dismissal, 10. Make Redundant.

A. The processes and methods used to transform tangible inputs (raw materials, semi-finished goods etc.) and intangible inputs (ideas, information, knowledge) into goods or services.

B. It is a business term that means a strict adherence to rules and regulations so that a procedure seems to take longer than necessary.

C. It shows how a group of people or professionals behave or should interact with each other.

D. A specific goal or purpose you attempt or intend to reach.

E. A good, idea, method, information, object or service created as a result of a process and serves a need or satisfies a want.

F. The volume of products that can be generated by a production plant or enterprise in a given period by using current resources.

G. The elimination of jobs or job categories caused by downsizing, rightsizing, or outsourcing.

H. A reasonably interchangeable good or material bought and sold freely as an article of commerce.

I. New market structures arising from digitalization, deregulation, globalization, and open-standards that are shifting the balance of economic power from the sellers to the buyers.

J. This is the termination of the contract of employment of an employee by his or her employer in a correct, fair, and lawful manner.

Choose the appropriate term, according to definition:

1. Based on individual discretion, not on objective criteria. Based on bias or prejudice, not on fact or reason
A. precedent
B. arbitrary
C. character
D. culture

2. Willing to help, liberal in giving or sharing, kind
A. to whisper
B. enormous
C. pension
D. competitor
E. generous

3. To own or have something
A. mine
B. to possess
C. to break down
D. department
E. to tackle

Choose the appropriate definition, according to the term:

4. **Feedback**
A. that can be legally used at a certain time; authoritative; well-founded
B. a time by which something need to be done
C. information, opinion about something (a product, idea, performance etc.)
D. extremely large; outrageous (enormous crimes)

5. **AUTOMATIC TELLER MACHINE (ATM)**
A. a device that gives access to financial transactions without the help of any worker
B. a field, usually a plain one, with grass and flowers
C. to consider what might be true but without being sure of it

D. money or gift that you give to somebody in order to achieve something

6. **Accounting**
A. feeling shame, sorrow, guilt about something
B. keeping a record of the money that a person or a company/organization earns and spend
C. to give something to somebody and get something from them
D. to be joined to something; to be fond of someone

7. **Purchase**
A. feeling shame, sorrow, guilt about something
B. keeping a record of the money that a person or a company/organization earns and spend
C. to give something to somebody and get something from them
D. to buy a product or service or product or service that has been bought by an individual or business.

8. **Procurement**
A. that can be legally used at a certain time; authoritative; well-founded
B. a time by which something needs to be done.
C. information, opinion about something (a product, idea, performance etc.)
D. act of obtaining or buying goods and services.

9. **Generally Accepted Accounting Principles (GAAP) are**
A. keeping records of the money that a person or a company earns and spend.
B. a time by which something need to be done
C. a common set of accounting principles, standards and procedures that companies use to compile their financial statements.
D. to buy a product or service or product or service that has been bought by an individual or a business.

10. **Demand**
A. an entire network of producers, distributors, and consumers of goods and services in a local, regional, or national community.
B. the total amount of funds which individuals or organizations want to commit for spending on goods or services over a specific period.

C. The total amount of a product (good or service) available for purchase at any specified price.

D. Approximation, prediction, or projection of a quantity based on experience and/or information available at the time, with the recognition that other pertinent facts are unclear or unknown.

21. CAPITALIZATION RATE

Meaning:
The capitalization rate is the rate of return on a real estate investment property based on the income that the property is expected to generate. The capitalization rate is used to estimate the investor's potential return on his or her investment. Capitalization Rate = Net Operating Income / Current Market Value and it is expressed in percentile.

Example:
Capitalization rate gives the first hand indicator of the investment worthiness of the asset. However, it is not an exhaustive measure by itself.

Now look it up to understand more, and then make your sentences.

1. _____.
2. _____.
3. _____.

22. BUSINESS ETHICS

Meaning:
This is the study of proper business policies and practices regarding potentially controversial issues, such as corporate governance, insider trading, bribery, discrimination, corporate social responsibility and fiduciary responsibilities.

Example:
Business people are often pressurized to behave unethically when seeking to make profits.

Now look it up to understand more, and then make your sentences.

1. _____.
2. _____.
3. _____.

23. FLEXIBLE SPENDING ACCOUNT

Meaning:
A benefit offered to an employee by an employer which allows a fixed amount of pre-tax wages to be set aside for qualified expenses. Qualified expenses may include child care or uncovered medical expenses. The amount set aside must be determined in advance and employees lose any unused dollars in the account at year-end.

Example:
Many employers offer their employees a flexible spending account to help pay for qualified medical expenses on a pre-tax basis.

Now look it up to understand more, and then make your sentences.

1. _____.
2. _____.
3. _____.

24. MICROECONOMICS

Meaning:
Microeconomics is the branch of economics that analyzes the market behavior of individual consumers and firms in an attempt tounderstand their decision-making process.

Example:
Breaking down other companies microeconomics can teach you a lot about how they run their business and what their goals are.

Now look it up to understand more, and then make your sentences.

1. _____.
2. _____.
3. _____.

25. MACROECONOMICS

Meaning:
Macroeconomics is concerned primarily with the forecasting of national income, through the analysis of major economic factors that show predictable patterns and trends, and of their influence on one another.

Example:
The knowledge of macroeconomics can be applied for large trends in buying and selling for products all over the world.

Now look it up to understand more, and then make your sentences.

1. _____.
2. _____.
3. _____.

26. ECONOMIC CYCLE

Meaning:
Recurring, fairly predictable, general pattern of periodic fluctuations (as measured by gross national product) in national economies.

Example:
Despite numerous attempts to explain causes of economic cycles, no theory is universally accepted or applicable.

Now look it up to understand more, and then make your sentences.

1. _____.
2. _____.
3. _____.

27. ASSETS

Meaning:
Assets are something that an entity has acquired or purchased, and that has money value (its cost, book value, market value, or residual value).

Meaning:
I told the hiring manager that due to my creativity and adaptability, I knew that I would be an important asset to the company.

Now look it up to understand more, and then make your sentences.

1. _____.
2. _____.
3. _____.

28. LIABILITY

Meaning:
Liability is a claim against the assets, or legal obligations of a person or organization, arising out of past or current transactions or actions. Liabilities require mandatory transfer of assets, or provision of services, at specified dates or in determinable future.

Example:
Winners of the contest have a liability to report and pay any taxes associated with the cash and material prizes awarded from the company.

Now look it up to understand more, and then make your sentences.

1. _____.
2. _____.
3. _____.

29. EQUITY

Meaning:
Equity implies giving as much advantage, consideration to one party as it is given to another.

Example:
Equity is essential for ensuring that extent and costs of funds, goods and services are fairly divided among their recipients.

Now look it up to understand more, and then make your sentences.

1. _____.
2. _____.
3. _____.

30. DEBTS

Meaning:
A duty or obligation to pay money, deliver goods, or render service under an express or implied agreement.

Example:
We analyzed our debt and decided we could leverage our company better if we efficiently take advantage of the opportunity.

Now look it up to understand more, and then make your sentences.

1. _____.
2. _____.
3. _____.

Treasure box 2: Economic cycle

> All market economies repeatedly (typically every five years) move through four stages; (1) expansion, (2) peak, (3) recession, and (4) recovery.

31. Credit

Meaning:
This is the ability to obtain goods, money, or services in return for a promise to pay at some later date.

Example:
You should have no trouble getting the loan if your credit is good.

Now look it up to understand other possible usage, and then make your sentences.

1. _____.
2. _____.
3. _____.

32. Cash basis accounting

Meaning:
An accepted form of accounting that records all revenues and expenditures at the time when payments are actually received or sent.

Example:
Cash basis accounting is appropriate for small or newer businesses that conduct business on a cash basis or that don't carry inventories.

Now look it up to understand more, and then make your sentences.

1. _____.
2. _____.
3. _____.

33. CASH IN SAVING

Meaning:
A deposit account at a bank or savings and loan which pays interest until a better alternative is found.

Example:
My grandmother refused to invest her money in the stock market and instead kept it all in a savings account at her bank where it would earn a little interest.

Now look it up to understand more, and then make your sentences.

1. _____.
2. _____.
3. _____.

34. CASH ON HAND

Meaning:
Funds that are immediately available to a business, and can be spent as needed, as opposed to assets that must be sold to generate cash

Example:
You should always make sure that you have enough cash on hand to take advantage of a good deal if it comes.

Now look it up to understand more, and then make your sentences.

1. _____.
2. _____.
3. _____.

35. ACCOUNTS RECEIVABLE

Meaning:
Money which is owed to a company by a customer for products and services provided on credit.

Example:
You need to make sure that you have good records of all of your accounts receivable so that you can know where your funds stand.

Now look it up to understand more, and then make your sentences.

1. _____.
2. _____.
3. _____.

36. ACCOUNT PAYABLE

Meaning:
Money which a company owes to vendors for products and services purchased on credit.

Example:
The company may be forced to file for bankruptcy as creditors were closing in because they have large sum of accounts payable.

Now look it up to understand more, and then make your sentences.

1. _____.
2. _____.
3. _____.

37. LIABILITY ACCOUNT/LOAN PAYABLE ACCOUNT

Meaning:
Accounting statement which tracks how much a person or business owes a creditor.

Example:
The liability account tracks debts owed to banks, vendors, employees and any other creditor who had not yet been paid for products or services received.

Now look it up to understand more, and then make your sentences.

1. _____.
2. _____.
3. _____.

38. CAPITAL

Meaning:
It may be defined as wealth in the form of money or assets, taken as a sign of the financial strength of an individual, organization, or nation, and assumed to be available for development or investment.

Example:
The small business owner needs an investment firm that is willing to give him the needed capital for his start-up business.

Now look it up to understand more, and then make your sentences.

1. _____.
2. _____.
3. _____.

39. INVENTORY

Meaning:
Is a list of materials and goods held by an organization to support production or for support activities or for sale or customer service such as merchandise, finished goods, and spare parts.

Example:
The inventory was stocked full last May but now it is depleted so we must contact our supplier.

Now look it up to understand more, and then make your sentences.

1. _____.
2. _____.
3. _____.

40. COPYRIGHT (©)

Meaning:
Copyright is the Legal monopoly that protects published or unpublished original work (usually for the duration of its author's life plus 50 years) from unauthorized duplication without due credit and compensation.

Example:
John wanted to upload his vacation videos to YouTube, but every time he tried, they kept getting taken down because of copyright violations, due to the music that was playing in the background.

Now look it up to understand more, and then make your sentences.

1. _____.
2. _____.
3. _____.

REVIEW QUIZ

1. The small business owner needs an investment firm that is willing to give him the needed............. for his start-up business.

2. Business people are often pressurized to behave .... when seeking to make profits.

3. Many employers offer their employees a.............. spending account to help pay for qualified medical expenses on a pre-tax basis

4. Winners of the contest have a................ to report and pay any taxes associated with the cash and material prizes awarded from the company.

5. John wanted to upload his vacation videos to YouTube, but every time he tried, they kept getting taken down because of ....violations, due to the music that was playing in the background

6. Breaking down other companies.................. can teach you a lot about how they run their business and what their goals are.

7. You need to make sure that you have good records of all of your ....so that you can know where your funds stand.

8. The company may be forced to file for bankruptcy as creditors were closing

9. This rate gives the first hand indicator of the investment worthiness of the asset.

10. Despite numerous attempts to explain causes of ....no theory is universally accepted or applicable.

11. I told the hiring manager that due to my creativity and adaptability, I knew that I would be an important ....to the company.

12. ……………….. is essential for ensuring that extent and costs of funds, goods and services are fairly divided among their recipients.

13. We analyzed our………………. and decided we could leverage our company better if we efficiently take advantage of the opportunity.

14. You should have no trouble getting the loan if your …………is good.

15. …………..accounting is appropriate for small or newer businesses that conduct cash based business or that don't carry inventories.

16. The knowledge of …………………..can be applied for large trends in buying and selling for products all over the world.

17. My grandmother refused to invest her money in the stock market and instead kept it all in a…………. at her bank where it would earn a little interest.

18. You should always make sure that you have enough ……………………………….
    to take advantage of a good deal if it comes.

    in because they have large sum of …………………….

19. The …………………tracks debts owed to banks, vendors, employees and any other creditor who had not yet been paid for products or services received.

20. The……………. was stocked full last May but now it is depleted so we must contact our supplier.

41. ETHICAL

Meaning:
This is an Equitable, fair, and just dealing with people that, although pragmatically flexible according to the situation and times, conform to self-imposed high standards of public conduct. Once practically interchangeable with 'moral'.

Example:
Ethical treatment of animals is a very controversial issue these days because some people do not think that products should be tested on animals prior to their sale.

Now look it up to understand more, and then make your sentences.

1. _____.
2. _____.
3. _____.

42. REMUNERATION

Meaning:
Reward for employment in the form of pay, salary, or wage, including allowances, benefits (such as company car, medical plan, and pension plan), bonuses, cash incentives, and monetary value of the noncash incentives.

Example:
The new employee was very pleased by the considerable remuneration his position at the company afforded him and was already planning what he should buy with it.

Now look it up to understand more, and then make your sentences.

1. _____.
2. _____.
3. _____.

43. Inherent

Meaning:
Inherent is the Essence, mechanism, or property that may not be evident from what is visible but underlies it and has to be inferred.

Example:
The inherent idea behind a bank is that they provide services for their members, and that has significantly changed over the years.

Now look it up to understand more, and then make your sentences.

1. _____.
2. _____.
3. _____.

44. Procurement

Meaning:
This is the act of obtaining or buying goods and services. The process includes preparation and processing of a demand as well as the end receipt and approval of payment.

Example:
A business will not be able to survive if its price of procurement is more than the profit it makes on selling the actual product.

Now look it up to understand more, and then make your sentences.

1. _____.
2. _____.
3. _____.

45. PURCHASE

Meaning:
Purchase is to buy a product or service by an individual or a business.

Example:
Sometimes a major purchase will cost a whole lot of money and it will be up to an individual or organization to figure out if it's worth it.

Now look it up to understand more, and then make your sentences.

1. _____.

2. _____.

3. _____.

TREASURE BOX 3: PROCUREMENTS

Procurements often involve;
(1) Purchase planning,
(2) Standards determination,
(3) Specifications development,
(4) Supplier research and selection,
(5) Value analysis,
(6) Financing,
(7) Price negotiation,
(8) Making the purchase,
(9) Supply contract administration,
(10) Inventory control and stores, and
(11) Disposals and other related functions.

46. Generally Accepted Accounting Principles (GAAP)

Meaning:
Generally Accepted Accounting Principles (GAAP) are a common set of accounting principles, standards and procedures that companies use to compile their financial statements.

Example:
GAAP are a combination of authoritative standards and simply the commonly accepted ways of recording and reporting accounting information.

Now look it up to understand more, and then make your sentences.

1. _____.
2. _____.
3. _____.

47. Reference

Meaning:
Reference is an individual that serves as the point of contact for employers seeking to verify or ask questions about a potential employee's background, work experience, or work ethic. An applicant may provide both professional and personal references to a potential employer.

Example:
I'm going to use my buddy Chris as a reference because he knows how reliable I am when I'm at work.

Now look it up to understand more, and then make your sentences.

1. _____.
2. _____.
3. _____.

48. PARTNERSHIP AGREEMENT

Meaning:
Written agreement between two or more individuals who join as partners to form and carry on a for-profit business. Among other things, it states the (1) nature of the business, (2) capital contributed by each partner, and (3) their rights and responsibilities.

Example:
They finally had a partnership agreement with each other and I was relieved because they had butted heads for long enough.

Now look it up to understand more, and then make your sentences.

1. _____.
2. _____.
3. _____.

49. BUNDLING

Meaning:
Bundling in marketing means the technique of offering two or more complementary goods or services together as a package deal. Bundled items are sold at a price attractively lower than the total of their individual selling prices. It is also called **price bundling**.

Example:
By bundling both premium cable television and high speed internet in a single package, the company was able to maintain high sales in both sectors.

Now look it up to understand more, and then make your sentences.

1. _____.
2. _____.
3. _____.

50. Passive incomes

Meaning:
Earnings from rent, limited partnership, or other sources of income in which the earner does not take an active part, not including salary, wage, interest, or capital gain. It is also called unearned income.

Example:
You can always include your passive income to your net worth.

Now look it up to understand more, and then make your sentences.

1. _____.
2. _____.
3. _____.

51. Recall

Meaning:
In finance, it means removal or withdrawal of a contaminated or defective good from sale by its manufacturer or producer, either voluntarily or when forced by a watchdog agency. Sometimes a good (such as a motor vehicle) is recalled after it has been sold, for rectification, exchange, or refund.

Example:
The automaker recalled one of its popular products due to numerous complaints by their users.

Now look it up to understand more, and then make your sentences.

1. _____.
2. _____.
3. _____.

52. BUDGET

Meaning:
This is an estimate, often itemized, of expected income and expense of a country, company, etc., and a plan of operations based on such an estimate for a given period in the future.

Example:
The budget was set and we could not alter our figures because we were held accountable by the CEO.

Now look it up to understand more, and then make your sentences.

1. _____.
2. _____.
3. _____.

53. STATEMENT OF ACCOUNT

Meaning:
Report released (on a fixed date every month) by banks that lists deposits, withdrawals, checks paid, interest earned, and service charges or penalties incurred on an account.
It may also mean a document, issued by a supplier to its customer, listing transactions over a given period, normally monthly.

Example:
If you are unsure of what your balance is you can find out when they send out the next bank statement that breaks down your account.

Now look it up to understand more, and then make your sentences.

1. _____.
2. _____.
3. _____.

54. CASH FLOWS

Meaning:
These are incomings and outgoings of cash, representing the operating activities of an organization.

Example:
An accountant must keep very detailed records of all the cash flow to know just how the business is doing.

Now look it up to understand more, and then make your sentences.

1. _____.
2. _____.
3. _____.

55. PRO FORMA STATEMENTS

Meaning:
A pro forma financial statement is one based on certain assumptions and projections in an attempt to present a reasonably accurate idea of what a firm's financial situation would be if the present trends continue.

Example:
Investors should be careful when reading a company's pro-forma financial statements, as the figures may not comply with generally accepted accounting principles (GAAP).

Now look it up to understand more, and then make your sentences.

1. _____.
2. _____.
3. _____.

56. COST OF PRODUCTION

Meaning:
The costs related to making or acquiring goods and services that directly generates revenue for a firm.

Example:
The company went bankrupt because rent, utilities, supplies and the high cost of production in general made their product too expensive for the average consumer.

Now look it up to understand more, and then make your sentences.

1. _____.
2. _____.
3. _____.

57. FUNDING

Meaning:
Funding is to allocate or provide funds for a program, project, etc.

Example:
You may need to have a special fund on the side that is always ready to buy up a lot of a resource if it becomes available.

Now look it up to understand more, and then make your sentences.

1. _____.
2. _____.
3. _____.

58. DIVERSIFICATION

Meaning:
This is the act or practice of manufacturing a variety of products, investing in a variety of securities, selling a variety of merchandise, etc., so that a failure in or an economic slump affecting one of them will not be disastrous.

Example:
The diversification of funds was a great choice made our financial department so we diversified our wealth intelligently and profitably.

Now look it up to understand more, and then make your sentences.

1. _____.
2. _____.
3. _____.

59. LIQUIDITY

Meaning:
A measure of the extent to which a person or organization has cash to meet immediate and short-term obligations, or assets that can be quickly converted to do this.

Example:
The bosses were quick to take advantage of the firm's current liquidity and spent almost all of it immediately redecorating the executive suites, gym, conference areas and dining room.

Now look it up to understand more, and then make your sentences.

1. _____.
2. _____.
3. _____.

60. LIQUIDATION

Meaning:
This means winding up of a firm by selling off its free (un-pledged) assets to convert them into cash to pay the firm's unsecured creditors.

Example:
In its final months as a functioning business, the video rental store had to turn to massive stock liquidation as a means to cover as many existing debts as possible before closing their doors for good.

Now look it up to understand more, and then make your sentences.

1. _____.
2. _____.
3. _____.

REVIEW QUIZ

1. In its final months as a functioning business, the video rental store had to turn to massive stock............... as a means to cover as many existing debts as possible before closing their doors for good.

2. A business will not be able to survive if its price of ....is more than the profit it makes on selling the actual product.

3. Investors should be careful when reading a company's .... financial statements, as the figures may not comply with generally accepted accounting principles (GAAP).

4. Sometimes a major ....will cost a whole lot of money and it will be up to an individual or organization to figure out if it's worth it.

5. The ....of funds was a great choice made our financial department so we diversified our wealth intelligently and profitably.

6. I'm going to use my buddy Chris as a ....because he knows how reliable I am when I'm at work.

7. They finally had a ....with each other and I was relieved because they had butted heads for long enough

8. By ....both premium cable television and high speed internet in a single package, the company was able to maintain high sales in both sectors.

9. You can always include your................. to your net worth.

10. The............. was set and we could not alter our figures because we were held accountable by the CEO.

11. If you are unsure of what your balance is you can find out when your bank sends out the next.................that breaks down your account.

12. .... are a combination of authoritative standards and simply the commonly accepted ways of recording and reporting accounting information.

13. An accountant must keep very detailed records of all the .... to know just how the business is doing.

14. The ....idea behind a bank is that they provide services for their members, and that has significantly changed over the years.

15. The company went bankrupt because rent, utilities, supplies and the high ....in general made their product too expensive for the average consumer.

16. .... treatment of animals is a very controversial issue these days because some people do not think that products should be tested on animals prior to their sale.

17. The automaker ....one of its popular products due to numerous complaints by their users.

18. The new employee was very pleased by the considerable ....his position at the company afforded him and was already planning what he should buy with it.

19. You may need to have a special ....on the side that is always ready to buy up a lot of a resource if it becomes available.

20. The bosses were quick to take advantage of the firm's current .... and spent almost all of it immediately redecorating the executive suites, gym, conference areas and dining room.

TREASURE BOX 4: BUSINESS ENGLISH

> Business English includes skills such as speaking on the telephone, creating a résumé or CV, writing emails and letters, making presentations, sales and Marketing. Understanding and correctly using business lingo with colleagues, customers and rival businesses will make you feel like a team player, a trusted and loyal part of the team/group.

61. BENEFIT

Meaning:
Desirable and measurable outcome or result or profit from an action, investment, project, resource, or technology.

Example:
We were able to benefit from our insurance policy in several ways when our house flooded in the massive floods last year.

Now look it up to understand more, and then make your sentences.

1. _____.
2. _____.
3. _____.

62. BENEFICIARY

Meaning:
A beneficiary is simply the recipient of money or other benefits.

Example:
When signing up for my life insurance policy I listed my daughter as my beneficiary so she could use the funds to settle any debts.

Now look it up to understand more, and then make your sentences.

1. _____.
2. _____.
3. _____.

63. FEEDBACK

Meaning:
Feedback is the return of information about the result of a process or activity.

Example:
We were always allowed to give feedback, bad or good, when our team attempted a new endeavor because it helped to improve things.

Now look it up to understand more, and then make your sentences.

1. _____.
2. _____.
3. _____.

64. PRODUCTIVITY

Meaning:
The rate at which goods or services are produced especially output per unit of labor.

Example:
The productivity of the individual was unmatched in the department so we decided to keep him during the layoffs.

Now look it up to understand more, and then make your sentences.

1. _____.
2. _____.
3. _____.

65. MARKETING

Meaning:
The strategic functions involved in identifying and appealing to particular groups of consumers, often including activities such as advertising, branding, pricing, and sales.

Example:
It was evident that carefully managed and created marketing would be needed to sell the new product.

Now look it up to understand more, and then make your sentences.

1. _____.
2. _____.
3. _____.

66. NEEDS

Meaning:
Needs is the driver of human action which marketers try to identify, emphasize, and satisfy, and around which promotional efforts are organized.

Example:
Sometimes your business may have a strong need for a product but don't go for one too strong or you won't get a fair price.

Now look it up to understand more, and then make your sentences.

1. _____.
2. _____.
3. _____.

67. WANTS

Meaning:
To want is to be deficient by the absence of some part or thing, or to feel or have a desire for something.

Example:
In the world of business, many people want to be promoted to a higher level to make more money and have more job security.

Now look it up to understand more, and then make your sentences.

1. _____.
2. _____.
3. _____.

68. CONSUMER SATISFACTION

Meaning:
Consumer satisfaction is the degree of satisfaction provided by the goods or services of a company as measured by the number of repeat customers.

Example:
My company was rated as the top store in customer satisfaction and had no complaints from customers over the last four months.

Now look it up to understand more, and then make your sentences.

1. _____.
2. _____.
3. _____.

69. MARKETING STRATEGY

Meaning:
It is an organization's strategy that combines all of its marketing goals into one comprehensive plan.

Example:
A good marketing strategy should be drawn from market research and focus on the right product mix in order to achieve the maximum profit potential and sustain the business.

Now look it up to understand more, and then make your sentences.

1. _____.
2. _____.
3. _____.

70. OPPORTUNITY COST

Meaning:
A benefit, profit, or value of something that must be given up to acquire or achieve something else. Since every resource (land, money, time, etc.) can be put to alternative uses, every action, choice, or decision has an associated opportunity cost.

Example:
The CEO of ABC Corporation declined the merger that the competing company offered him after examining the opportunity cost and realized that the sacrifices were too high compared with the very low benefits to accept the deal.

Now look it up to understand more, and then make your sentences.

1. _____.
2. _____.
3. _____.

71. MARKET DEVELOPMENT

Meaning:
The expansion of the total market for a product or company by (1) entering new segments of the market, (2) converting nonusers into users, and/or (3) increasing usage per user.

Example:
You should always have a strong market development team on your side to get the most out of your product.

Now look it up to understand more, and then make your sentences.

1. _____.
2. _____.
3. _____.

72. PRODUCT DEVELOPMENT

Meaning:
This is the creation of products with new or different characteristics that offer new or additional benefits to the customer.

Example:
Proper product development ensures the end product will support all requirements while meeting all codes required of particular type of product.

Now look it up to understand more, and then make your sentences.

1. _____.
2. _____.
3. _____.

73. MARKET PENETRATION

Meaning:
The activity or fact of increasing the market share of an existing product, or promoting a new product, through strategies such as bundling, advertising, lower prices, or volume discounts.

Example:
The market penetration generated by the new strategy was effective and our next quarter's profits reflected the positive change for us.

Now look it up to understand more, and then make your sentences.

1. _____.
2. _____.
3. _____.

74. COMPETITORS

Meaning:
Competitor is any person or entity or business, a company in the same industry or a similar industry which offers a similar product or service.

Example:
The presence of one or more competitors can reduce the prices of goods and services as the companies attempt to gain a larger market share.

Now look it up to understand more, and then make your sentences.

1. _____.
2. _____.
3. _____.

75. FINANCIAL CAPITAL

Meaning:
Financial capital is funds provided by lenders (and investors) to businesses to purchase real capital equipment for producing goods/services.

Example:
You should always know how much financial capital you have so that you can budget your books according to it.

Now look it up to understand more, and then make your sentences.

1. _____.
2. _____.
3. _____.

TREASURE BOX 5: SAY WOW! NOT WHY? NOT HOW?

When you are learning English or even any other languages and you come across something new or different, be excited about the new discovery so to speak and accept it with pure heart. Although, you may need to check more deeply for more information or for more understanding on that new vocabulary, business term or word and phrase soon or later.

76. DISTRIBUTION INTENSITY

Meaning:
The level of a product's availability in a market selected by a marketer.

Example:
The level of distribution intensity the marketer chooses is often dependent on factors such as the size of the target market, pricing and promotion and production capacity, in addition to the amount of service the product will need after its purchase if applicable.

Now look it up to understand more, and then make your sentences.

1. _____.
2. _____.
3. _____.

77. SALES AND MARKET RESEARCH

Meaning:
Sales and Market research is the identification of a specific market and measurement of its size and other characteristics and analyzing sales resultsand studying the effectiveness of sales promotions.

Example:
If a company's marketing research shows an increase in demand for their top level product, they would be foolish to discontinue the manufacturing and sales of that product.

Now look it up to understand more, and then make your sentences.

1. _____.
2. _____.
3. _____.

78. ADVERTISING RESEARCH

Meaning:
A research conducted to improve the efficiency of an advertisement focused on one particular advertisement or in general to know the impact of advertising on consumer behavior and to know the competitors' ad and how it is portrayed.

Example:
The focus of ad research is on what the advertising has done for the brand, such as increasing thebrand awareness, trial and/or frequency of purchasing.

Now look it up to understand more, and then make your sentences.

1. _____.
2. _____.
3. _____.

79. PRODUCT RESEARCH

Meaning:
Product research includes analyzing new product potential and its acceptance in the market and analyzing the competitive product.

Example:
Product research is a very important activity in new product development.

Now look it up to understand more, and then make your sentences.

1. _____.

2. _____.

3. _____.

80. MARKET ANALYSIS

Meaning:
This is the detailed examination and report of a market which include information about the industry, target market, competition and how the company intends to make a place for its products and services.

Example:
A market analysis should be an integral part of and within a special industry.

Now look it up to understand more, and then make your sentences.

1. _____.

2. _____.

3. _____.

REVIEW QUIZ

1. We were able to……….. from our insurance policy in several ways when our house flooded in the massive floods last year.

2. When signing up for my life insurance policy I listed my daughter as my …………….so she could use the funds to settle any debts.

3. You should always have a strong …………….team on your side to get the most out of your product.

4. Proper ………….ensures the end product will support all requirements while meeting all codes required of particular type of product.

5. The …………….of the individual was unmatched in the department so we decided to keep him during the layoffs.

6. In the world of business, many people……….. to be promoted to a higher level to make more money and have more job security.

7. The CEO of ABC Corporation declined the merger that the competing company offered him after examining the …………….and realized that the sacrifices were too high compared with the very low benefits to accept the deal.

8. The …………….generated by the new strategy was effective and our next quarter's profits reflected the positive change for us.

9. The presence of one or more …………..can reduce the prices of goods and services as the companies attempt to gain a larger market share.

10. The level of …………….the marketer chooses is often dependent on factors such as the size of the target market, pricing and promotion and production

capacity, in addition to the amount of service the product will need after its purchase if applicable.

11. My company was rated as the top store in ....and had no complaints from customers over the last four months.

12. We were always allowed to give..............., bad or good, when our team attempted a new endeavor because it helped to improve things.

13. A ....should be an integral part of and within a special industry.

14. It was evident that carefully managed and created............. would be needed to sell the new product.

15. A good............... should be drawn from market research and focus on the right product mix in order to achieve the maximum profit potential and sustain the business.

16. Sometimes your business may have a strong ....for a product but don't go for one too strong or you won't get a fair price.

17. If a company's ....shows an increase in demand for their top level product, they would be foolish to discontinue the manufacturing and sales of that product.

18. .... is a very important activity in new product development.

19. You should always know how much........... you have so that you can budget your books according to it.

20. The focus of ....is on what the advertising has done for the brand, such as increasing the brand awareness, trial and/or frequency of purchasing.

81. CONSUMER BEHAVIOR

Meaning:
The process by which individuals search for, select, purchase, use, and dispose of goods and services, in satisfaction of their needs and wants.

Example:
The study of consumer behavior is fundamental to the understanding of the demand-side of the market.

Now look it up to understand more, and then make your sentences.

1. _____.
2. _____.
3. _____.

82. MICROENVIRONMENT

Meaning:
The factors or elements in an organization's immediate area of operations such as competitors, customers, distribution channels, suppliers, and the general public, that affect its performance and decision-making freedom.

Example:
Microenvironment is one of the key elements to the marketing environment.

Now look it up to understand more, and then make your sentences.

1. _____.
2. _____.
3. _____.

83. MACRO ENVIRONMENT

Meaning:
The major external and uncontrollable factors such as, the economic factors;demographics; legal, political, and social conditions; technological changes; and natural forces that influence an organization's decision making, and affect its performance and strategies.

Example:
You should always be prepared to handle anything that a macro environment can throw at you quickly and swiftly to keep our business afloat and alive.

Now look it up to understand more, and then make your sentences.

1. _____.
2. _____.
3. _____.

84. ENVIRONMENTAL FACTORS

Meaning:
This is an identifiable element in the physical, cultural, demographic, economic, political, regulatory, or technological environment that affects the survival, operations, and growth of an organization.

Example:
There can be many different environmental factors that will make a big impact on how a product plays out in some market areas.

Now look it up to understand more, and then make your sentences.

1. _____.
2. _____.
3. _____.

85. INNOVATION

Meaning:
This is the process of translating an idea or invention into a good or services either Evolutionary innovation or revolutionary, that creates value or for which consumers will pay.

Example:
By allowing the developer of an innovation to reap the rewards of his efforts, we create an environment that encourages innovative thinking and hard work.

Now look it up to understand more, and then make your sentences.

1. _____.
2. _____.
3. _____.

86. INNOVATORS

Meaning:
Innovators are the first people to try or introduce new ideas, processes, goods and services into an environment.

Example:
In all new markets, there are three types of firms: the innovators, the imitators, and the idiots.

Now look it up to understand more, and then make your sentences.

1. _____.
2. _____.
3. _____.

87. MEASURING AND FORECASTING DEMAND

Meaning:
This is the act of predicting the size and potential of business activity for a future period of time based upon specific assumptions, such as targeted prospects or a defined sales strategy.

Example:
The CEO hoped his executive team would be encouraged by the generally positive business forecast laid out by the financial department.

Now look it up to understand more, and then make your sentences.

1. _____.
2. _____.
3. _____.

88. FULFILLMENT

Meaning:
Fulfillment is the process of taking an order and executing it, whichmay involve warehouse pickup, packaging, labeling, etc. by making it ready for delivery to its intended customer.

Example:
The manager of the paper company oversaw the warehouse's fulfillment of the order because the warehouse workers were known to slack off.

Now look it up to understand more, and then make your sentences.

1. _____.
2. _____.
3. _____.

89. RESELLER MARKET

Meaning:
This is the market where buyers who purchase with the intent of selling those products to others. The reseller market includes wholesalers, retailers, and distributors. Resellers may restrict their purchases to one product or brand or offer a variety of products and brands.

Example:
Resellers may take stock or they may simply process orders through a website or by phone.

Now look it up to understand more, and then make your sentences.

1. _____.
2. _____.
3. _____.

90. BRAND

Meaning:
Brand is a distinctive name, term, sign, symbol or design used to identify a firm's product and to distinguish it from similar products offered by competitors.

Example:
The business submitted requests for a new logo and brand design, to enhance their appeal to the consumer both visually and conceptually.

Now look it up to understand more, and then make your sentences.

1. _____.
2. _____.
3. _____.

TREASURE BOX 6: KNOW YOURSELF

Discover yourself! When you know yourself or know your personality or your intelligence, then you will study the right way and excel. Here are Different types of intelligences.

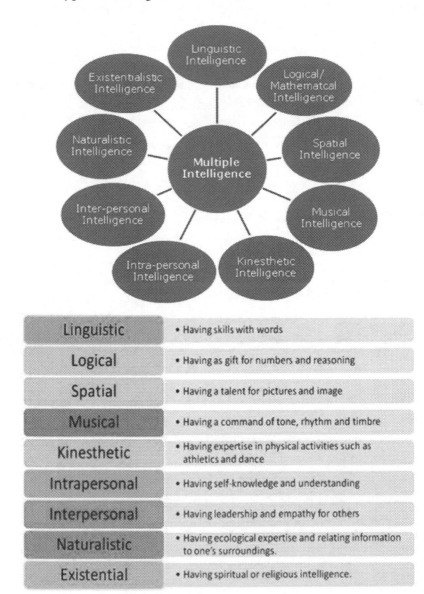

Linguistic	• Having skills with words
Logical	• Having as gift for numbers and reasoning
Spatial	• Having a talent for pictures and image
Musical	• Having a command of tone, rhythm and timbre
Kinesthetic	• Having expertise in physical activities such as athletics and dance
Intrapersonal	• Having self-knowledge and understanding
Interpersonal	• Having leadership and empathy for others
Naturalistic	• Having ecological expertise and relating information to one's surroundings.
Existential	• Having spiritual or religious intelligence.

Where do you belong? You may have more than one though.

91. BRANDING

Meaning:
Branding is the process of creating differentiation between a product and other products of the same kind.

Example:
Branding is a marketing strategy to create the impression that one product is better than the other, whether it is true or not.

Now look it up to understand more, and then make your sentences.

1. _____.
2. _____.
3. _____.

92. BRAND NAME

Meaning:
Brand name is a word or words widely known and that identify not only a product but also its manufacturer or producer.

Example:
I recognized the brand name immediately and it made me think back to when I was a kid.

Now look it up to understand more, and then make your sentences.

1. _____.
2. _____.
3. _____.

93. PACKAGING

Meaning:
Processes (such as cleaning, drying, and preserving) and materials (such as glass, metal, paper or paperboard, plastic) employed to contain, handle, protect, and/or transport an article.
Note: Package is also a bundle of something, usually of small or medium size, that is packed and wrapped or boxed; parcel.

Example:
The packaging used was carefully selected by our research and development team so that it is appealing when people see it in the store.

Now look it up to understand more, and then make your sentences.

1. _____.
2. _____.
3. _____.

94. PRODUCT LIFE CYCLE

Meaning:
It is the journey of a product from "new and exciting" to "old and dated."

Example:
If you want topurchase a product or invest in a business, first you need to figure out the product life cycle to prevent losing a large sum of money.

Now look it up to understand more, and then make your sentences.

1. _____.
2. _____.
3. _____.

95. ADVERTISING

Meaning:
Advertising is the activity or profession of producing information for promoting the sale of commercial products or services.

Example:
I work for an advertising agency, who designs, creates and sells online ads for kids' toys, games, electronics and books.

Now look it up to understand more, and then make your sentences.

1. _____.
2. _____.
3. _____.

96. DISTRIBUTION

Meaning:
Distribution in commerce is the movement of goods and services from the source through a distribution channel, right up to the final consumer, or user, and the movement of payment in the opposite direction, right up to the original producer or supplier.

Example:
You need to have a great distribution team on hand so that your product gets to its customers on time always.

Now look it up to understand more, and then make your sentences.

1. _____.
2. _____.
3. _____.

97. Distribution system

Meaning:
Entire set-up consisting of procedures, methods, equipment, and facilities, designed and interconnected to facilitate and monitor the flow of goods or services from the source to the end user.

Example:
Within a distribution system we can find multiple channels to enable distribution

Now look it up to understand more, and then make your sentences.

1. _____.
2. _____.
3. _____.

98. Distribution channels

Meaning:
The path through which goods and services travel from the vendor to the consumer or payments for those products travel from the consumer to the vendor.

Example:
You need to know the right distribution channel and how to effectively use it to get the most out of your product.

Now look it up to understand more, and then make your sentences.

1. _____.
2. _____.
3. _____.

99. SUBSIDY

Meaning:
Economic benefit or financial aid provided by a government to support a desirable activity, such as keeping prices of staples low, maintaining the income of the producers of critical or strategic products, maintaining employment levels, or inducing investment to reduce unemployment.

Example:
For decades, the federal government has provided a subsidy to corn producers in order to lower the price of corn and products containing corn for consumers.

Now look it up to understand more, and then make your sentences.

1. _____.
2. _____.
3. _____.

100. AUTONOMOUS INVESTMENT'

Meaning:
An autonomous investment consists of expenditures in a country or region that is independent of economic growth. They are investments made for the good of society and not for the goal of making profits. Autonomous investment is the opposite of **induced investment.**

Example:
Autonomous investments, such as building of roads and highways, keep the economic engine running.

Now look it up to understand more, and then make your sentences.

1. _____.
2. _____.
3. _____.

Review Quiz

1. The study of ....is fundamental to the understanding of the demand-side of the market.

2. There can be many different............... that will make a big impact on how a product plays out in some market areas.

3. .... is a marketing strategy to create the impression that one product is better than the other, whether it is true or not.

4. For decades, the federal government has provided a...................... to corn producers in order to lower the price of corn and products containing corn for consumers.

5. ....such as building of roads and highways, keep the economic engine running.

6. ....may take stock or they may simply process orders through a website or by phone.

7. By allowing the developer of an ....to reap the rewards of his efforts, we create an environment that encourages innovative thinking and hard work.

8. In all new markets, there are three types of firms: the ....the imitators, and the idiots.

9. The CEO hoped his executive team would be encouraged by the generally positive business.................... laid out by the financial department,

10. The manager of the paper company oversaw the warehouse's .... of the order because the warehouse workers were known to slack off.

11. The ....used was carefully selected by our research and development team so that it is appealing when people see it in the store.

12. The business submitted requests for a new logo and..................... design, to enhance their appeal to the consumer both visually and conceptually.

13. I recognized the ....immediately and it made me think back to when I was a kid.

14. If you want to purchase a product or invest in a business, first you need to figure out the product............. to prevent losing a large sum of money.

15. ....is one of the key elements to the marketing environment.

16. I work for an........................., which designs, creates and sells online ads for kids' toys, games, electronics and books.

17. You should always be prepared to handle anything that a ....can throw at you quickly and swiftly to keep your business afloat and alive.

18. Within a ....we can find multiple channels to enable distribution

19. You need to have a great ....team on hand so that your product gets to its customers on time always.

20. You need to know the right ....and how to effectively use it to get the most out of your product.

101. INDUCED INVESTMENT

Meaning:
Investment effected by a growing national economy that stimulates demand. As output levels rise, capacity utilization increases resulting in additional capital investment.

Example:
Induced investment is undertaken in response to consumers' demand for a producer's goods.

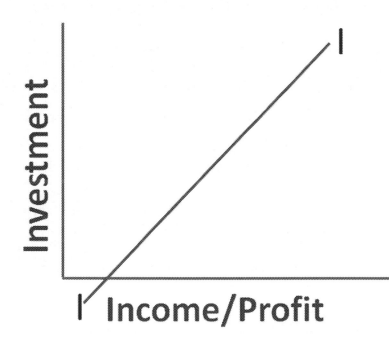

Now look it up to understand more, and then make your sentences.

1. _____.
2. _____.
3. _____.

102. CAPITALISM

Meaning:
Economic system based (to a varying degree) on private ownership of the factors of production (capital, land, and labor) employed in generation of profits.

Example:
Capitalism is the oldest and most common of all economic systems and, in general, is synonymous with free market system.

Now look it up to understand more, and then make your sentences.

1. _____.
2. _____.
3. _____.

103. MONOPOLY

Meaning:
Monopoly is the market situation where one producer (or a group of producers acting in concert) controls supply of a good or service, and where the entry of new producers is prevented or highly restricted.

Example:
The company had achieved such total dominance in its area of the market that it had effectively become a monopoly, making it impossible for competitors to succeed.

Now look it up to understand more, and then make your sentences.

1. _____.
2. _____.
3. _____.

104. WHOLESALING

Meaning:
Wholesaling is the business of selling goods and services in large amounts to other businesses rather than to individual customers.

Example:
Wholesaling is one step on the supply chain, which includes various companies like suppliers, manufacturers and retailers.

Now look it up to understand more, and then make your sentences.

1. _____.
2. _____.
3. _____.

105. RETAILING

Meaning:
Retailing is the business of selling goods and services to ultimate consumers for personal or household consumption.

Example:
The company branched out from car retailing into car leasing.

Now look it up to understand more, and then make your sentences.

1. _____.
2. _____.
3. _____.

TREASURE BOX 7: INDEPENDENT STUDY

Studies have shown that personality can influence whether a person enjoys an independent study project, rather than lectures. However, people that believe the teacher should be authoritarian did not perform well in independent studies. You need the ability of independent study to excel in your carrier, remember you still need to interact to be able to put into practice what you have learned without which you cannot connect..

106. STRATEGIC ALLIANCE

Meaning:
Strategic alliance is an agreement between two or more individuals or entities stating that the involved parties will act in a certain way in order to achieve a common goal. Strategic alliances usually make sense when the parties involved have complementary strengths.

Example:
The strategic alliance allowed the whole to be greater than the sum of its parts as each individual contributed significant resources."

Now look it up to understand more, and then make your sentences.

1. _____.
2. _____.
3. _____.

107. SPLITTING UP

Meaning:
A strategy adopted by corporates in which a single incorporated organization splits into two or more companies which are then run separately.

Example:
Splitting up of a company generally happens for corporate strategic reasons or because the government makes it compulsory.

Now look it up to understand more, and then make your sentences.

1. _____.
2. _____.
3. _____.

108. MERGER

Meaning:
Merger is the act or process of combining two or more businesses into one, through a purchase acquisition or a pooling of interests.

Example:
You may want to have a merger with another company if you think that will be the best thing for you.

Now look it up to understand more, and then make your sentences.

1. _____.
2. _____.
3. _____.

109. ARBITRAGE

Meaning:
Profiting from differences in prices or yields in different markets. 'Arbitrageurs' buy a commodity, currency, security or any other financial instrument in one place and immediately sell it at a higher price to a ready buyer at another place completing both ends of the transaction usually within a few seconds.

Example:
The day traders practiced the art of arbitrage with skill, buying and selling throughout the day with barely any break in activity.

Now look it up to understand more, and then make your sentences.

1. _____.

2. _____.

3. _____.

110. INFRASTRUCTURE

Meaning:
This is a relatively permanent and foundational capital investment of a country, firm, or project that underlies and makes possible all its economic activity. It includes administrative, telecommunications, transportation, utilities, and waste removal and processing facilities. Some definitions also include education, health care, research and development, and training facilities.

Example:
Whenever I return to Japan from a third world country, I am always impressed by its infrastructure, especially the roads and power grid, which are well-maintained and very reliable.

Now look it up to understand more, and then make your sentences.

1. _____.

2. _____.

3. _____.

111. GLOBAL MARKETING

Meaning:
This is the process of conceptualizing and then conveying a final product or service worldwide with the hopes of reaching the international marketing community.

Example:
You should be good at global marketing so that your business can expand into every possible market.

Now look it up to understand more, and then make your sentences.

1. _____.
2. _____.
3. _____.

112. GLOBALIZATION

Meaning:
Globalization is the tendency of investment funds and businesses to move beyond domestic and national markets to other markets around the globe, thereby increasing the interconnectedness of different markets.

Example:
The sharing of popular culture and entertainment of Japan and the United States as well as other countries is caused by increased globalization via the internet.

Now look it up to understand more, and then make your sentences.

1. _____.
2. _____.
3. _____.

113. EXCHANGE RATES

Meaning:
This is the Price for which the currency of a country can be exchanged for another country's currency.

Example:
When dealing in foreign affairs sometimes you will need to use a different currency and need to find the best exchange rate.

Now look it up to understand more, and then make your sentences.

1. _____.
2. _____.
3. _____.

114. MARKET NICHE

Meaning:
A small but profitable segment of a market suitable for focused attention by a marketer. Market niches do not exist by themselves, but are created by identifying needs or wants that are not being addressed by competitors, and by offering products that satisfy them.

Example:
The company should have a special niche in the marketplace.

Now look it up to understand more, and then make your sentences.

1. _____.
2. _____.
3. _____.

115. PRIMARY MARKET

Meaning:
This is a market in which buyers and sellers negotiate and transact business directly, without any intermediary such as resellers or a market in which newly issued securities are offered to the public.

Example:
When dealing in the primary market you must be a good negotiator to always get the best price you can.

Now look it up to understand more, and then make your sentences.

1. _____.
2. _____.
3. _____.

116. SECONDARY MARKET

Meaning:
This is where previously issued products, securities (such bonds, notes, and shares) and financial instruments (such as bills of exchange and certificates of deposit) are bought and sold.

Example:
You should always try to make sure that there are people in the secondary market that may also have need for your product.

Now look it up to understand more, and then make your sentences.

1. _____.
2. _____.
3. _____.

117. SUNK COST

Meaning:

A sunk cost is a past cost that has already been incurred and cannot be recovered and that is independent of any event or spending decision that may occur in the future.

Example:

Sometimes, you just have to admit that your project has failed and all of the money that you put into it is now a sunk cost.

Now look it up to understand more, and then make your sentences.

1. _____.
2. _____.
3. _____.

118. DIFFERENTIAL ANALYSIS

Meaning:

Also called incremental analysis or relevant cost analysis is a decision making method in which evaluation is confined to only those factors which are different or unique among possible alternatives.

Example:

Differential analysis usually involves selecting the alternative offering the best cost-to-benefit ratio among other factors.

Now look it up to understand more, and then make your sentences.

1. _____.
2. _____.
3. _____.

119. FINANCIAL LEVERAGE

Meaning:
Financial leverage is the use of borrowed money to increase production volume, and thus sales and earnings. It is measured as the **ratio of total debt** to **total assets**. The greater the amount of debt, the greater the financial leverage.

Example:
We thought we would have a lot more financial leverage with the money we borrowed and it would help us out.

Now look it up to understand more, and then make your sentences.

1. _____.
2. _____.
3. _____.

120. INTEREST RATE

Meaning:
Interest rate is the cost, usually expressed as a percentage per annum charged on money borrowed or lent. The interest rate may be variable or fixed.

Example:
Credit cards have an interest rate that works against the user while savings accounts have an interest rate that works for the user.

Now look it up to understand more, and then make your sentences.

1. _____.
2. _____.
3. _____.

TREASURE BOX 8: DON'T LEARN IN ISOLATION

Note that all these business terms or phrases and words do not occur in Isolation. They are always related in one way or another. Try as much as possible to associate them, and then you will see and appreciate their beauty, you will understand them more and connect well with them in your carrier.

REVIEW QUIZ

1. ....is one step on the supply chain, which includes various companies like suppliers, manufacturers and retailers

2. The.............. allowed the whole to be greater than the sum of its parts as each individual contributed significant resources."

3. ....up of a company generally happens for corporate strategic reasons or because the government makes it compulsory.

4. ....is undertaken in response to consumers' demand for a producer's goods.

5. The company.............. out from car retailing into car leasing.

6. ....is the oldest and most common of all economic systems and, in general, is synonymous with free market system.

7. The company had achieved such total dominance in its area of the market that it had effectively become a............... making it impossible for competitors to succeed.

8. Sometimes, you just have to admit that your project has failed and all of the money that you put into it is now a..............

9. You may want to have a.............. with another company if you think that will be the best thing for you.

10. You should be good at ....so that your business can expand into every possible market.

11. The sharing of popular culture and entertainment of Japan and the United States as well as other countries is caused by increased ……………..via the internet.

12. When dealing in the …………..you must be a good negotiator to always get the best price you can.

13. You should always try to make sure that there are people in the…………………. that may also have need for your product.

14. …………………usually involves selecting the alternative offering the best cost-to-benefit ratio among other factors.

15. The day traders practiced the art of …………….with skill, buying and selling throughout the day with barely any break in activity.

16. Whenever I return to Japan from a third world country, I am always impressed by its………………., especially the roads and power grid, which are well-maintained and very reliable.

17. We thought we would have a lot more financial…………. with the money we borrowed and it would help us out.

18. Credit cards have an interest rate that works against the user while savings accounts have an……………. that works for the user.

19. When dealing in ………………sometimes you will need to use a different currency and need to find the best exchange rate.

20. The company should have a special …………..in the marketplace.

121. MARKET PENETRATION PRICING

Meaning:
A strategy adopted for quickly achieving a high volume of sales and deep market penetration of a new product whereby it is widely promoted and its introductory price is kept comparatively low.

Example:
The disadvantage of penetration pricing is that, customers may leave the brand once prices begin to rise to levels more in line with competitors.

Now look it up to understand more, and then make your sentences.

1. _____.
2. _____.
3. _____.

122. MORTGAGE

Meaning:
A mortgage is a debt instrument, secured by the collateral of specified real estate property, which the borrower is obliged to pay back with a predetermined set of payments.

Example:
It is always important to make your payments on time and stay up to date to get rid of your mortgage as quick as possible.

Now look it up to understand more, and then make your sentences.

1. _____.
2. _____.
3. _____.

123. MORTGAGE MARKETS

Meaning:
Mortgage markets consist of ***primary mortgage market*** in which loans are originated and consisting of lenders such as commercial banks, savings and loan associations, and mutual savings banks often sold to the ***secondary mortgage market*** where they are resold.

Example:
The secondary mortgage market helps to make credit equally available to all borrowers across geographical locations.

Now look it up to understand more, and then make your sentences.

1. _____.
2. _____.
3. _____.

124. OLIGOPOLIES

Meaning:
A market dominated by a small number of participants who are able to collectively exert control over supply and market prices.

Example:
We've got to do something to find a way to break into this emerging market, because as it stands we've got an oligopoly on our hands."

Now look it up to understand more, and then make your sentences.

1. _____.
2. _____.
3. _____.

125. SWOT Analysis

Meaning:
SWOT analysis evaluates your company's strengths, weaknesses, market opportunities and potential threats to provide competitive insight into the potential and critical issues that impact the overall success of the business.

Example:
The primary goal of a SWOT analysis is to identify and assign all significant factors that could positively or negatively impact success to a business.

Now look it up to understand more, and then make your sentences.

1. _____.
2. _____.
3. _____.

126. Economy pricing

Meaning:
This is a valuation technique which assigns a low price to selected products widely used in the retail food business for groceries such as canned and frozen goods sold under generic food brands where marketing and production costs have been kept to a minimum.

Example:
The generic items are priced lower due to the fact that they require very little marketing and promotion expenses.

Now look it up to understand more, and then make your sentences.

1. _____.
2. _____.
3. _____.

127. FUTURES

Meaning:
Commodities or securities contracted for delivery at a stated future date at a specified price. Such a contract, called futures contract, itself can also be traded.

Example:
Investing in the futures of a company can be a risky venture but if you pick right you will reap the rewards.

Now look it up to understand more, and then make your sentences.

1. _____.
2. _____.
3. _____.

128. FINANCIAL INTELLIGENCE

Meaning:
Financial intelligence is the knowledge and skills gained from understanding finance and accounting principles in the business world.

Example:
Financial intelligence is not an innate skill; rather it is a learned set of skills that can be developed at all levels.

Now look it up to understand more, and then make your sentences.

1. _____.
2. _____.
3. _____.

129. BONDS

Meaning:
A bond is a debt investment in which an investor loans money to an entity (typically corporate or governmental) which borrows the funds for a defined period of time at a variable or fixed interest rate.

Example:
Many corporate and government bonds are publicly traded on exchanges, while others are traded only over-the-counter (OTC).

Now look it up to understand more, and then make your sentences.

1. _____.
2. _____.
3. _____.

130. STOCKS

Meaning:
A stock is a share of a company held by an individual or group. Corporations raise capital by issuing stocks and entitle the stock owners (shareholders) to partial ownership of the corporation. Stocks are bought and sold on what is called an exchange.

Examples:
Ex 1: I invest in shares and I've got some in France Telecom recently.
Ex 2: Share prices on New York Stock Exchange have risen considerably, so it's a good time to sell my shares.

Now look it up to understand more, and then make your sentences.

1. _____.
2. _____.
3. _____.

131. STOCK MARKET

Meaning:
The stock market is the market in which shares of publicly held companies are issued and traded either through exchanges or over-the-counter markets.

Example:
When companies are profitable, stock market investors make money through the dividends the companies pay out.

Now look it up to understand more, and then make your sentences.

1. _____.
2. _____.
3. _____.

132. COMMON STOCK

Meaning:
A common stock is a security that represents ownership in a corporation.

Example:
Holders of common stock exercise control by electing a board of directors and voting on corporate policy.

Now look it up to understand more, and then make your sentences.

1. _____.
2. _____.
3. _____.

133. MARKETABLE SECURITY

Meaning:
Equity or debt instrument (share/stock, bond, note) that is listed on an exchange and can be readily bought or sold.

Example:
My portfolio is comprised almost entirely of things that might be considered a marketable security, because I want to make sure I can liquidate them quickly, if need be.

Now look it up to understand more, and then make your sentences.

1. _____.
2. _____.
3. _____.

134. CONVERTIBLE SECURITIES

Meaning:
Bond, preferred stock, or debenture that is exchangeable at the option of the holder for common stock of the issuing corporation.

Example:
The performance of a convertible security is heavily influenced by the price of the underlying common stock.

Now look it up to understand more, and then make your sentences.

1. _____.
2. _____.
3. _____.

135. CORPORATION

Meaning:
Firm that meets certain legal requirements to be recognized as having a legal existence, as an entity separate and distinct from its owners. Corporations are owned by their stockholders (shareholders) who share in profits and losses generated through the firm's operations.

Example:
The shareholders of the corporation must include their yearly dividends as income when they file their taxes at the end of the year.

Now look it up to understand more, and then make your sentences.

1. _____.

2. _____.

3. _____.

TREASURE BOX 9: TRUST YOURSELF;

Do not doubt yourself or your ability in all things especially when you are learning English. To learn English and be fluent in English, you are and you have to be your best fan! You'll do more harm by doubting yourself than when other people doubt you.

136. CASH DISBURSEMENTS

Meaning:
Cash disbursements is the cash outflow or payment of money to settle obligations such as operating expenses, interest payments for loans and accounts receivables during a particular period in order to carry out business activities.

Example:
The new branch office relied on a regular cash disbursement from their parent corporation in order to handle setting up a new location.

Now look it up to understand more, and then make your sentences.

1. _____.
2. _____.
3. _____.

137. BUREAUCRACY

Meaning:
A system of administration distinguished by its, clear hierarchy of authority, rigid division of labor, written and inflexible rules, regulations, and procedures, and impersonal relationships.

Example:
Police officers, postal workers, city employees, and many other people who hold government positions are all part of a typical bureaucracy.

Now look it up to understand more, and then make your sentences.

1. _____.
2. _____.
3. _____.

138. DIVIDEND

Meaning:
A share of the after-tax profit of a company, distributed to its shareholders according to the number and class of shares held by them.

Example:
Dividend payments must be approved by the board of directors.

Now look it up to understand more, and then make your sentences.

1. _____.
2. _____.
3. _____.

139. SHAREHOLDER

Meaning:
An individual, group, or organization that owns one or more shares in a company and in whose name the share certificate is issued.

Example:
If you can keep your main shareholder happy then you will continue to have enough money to run your business properly.

Now look it up to understand more, and then make your sentences.

1. _____.
2. _____.
3. _____.

140. LIMITED LIABILITY

Meaning:
The legal protection available to the shareholders of privately and publicly owned corporations under which the financial liability of each shareholder for the company's debts and obligations is limited to the par value of his or her fully paid-up shares.

Example:
You should try to make sure that you have limited liability any time you are doing something that may be very risky.

Now look it up to understand more, and then make your sentences.

1. _____.
2. _____.
3. _____.

REVIEW QUIZ

1. The secondary …………helps to make credit equally available to all borrowers across geographical locations.

2. My portfolio is comprised almost entirely of things that might be considered a……………. because I want to make sure I can liquidate them quickly, if need be.

3. The generic items are ……………..lower due to the fact that they require very little marketing and promotion expenses.

4. We've got to do something to find a way to break into this emerging market, because as it stands we've got an ……………on our hands."

5. Investing in the …………..of a company can be a risky venture but if you pick right you will reap the rewards.

6. If you can keep your main ……………..happy then you will continue to have enough money to run your business properly.

7. When companies are profitable, ……………investors make money through the dividends the companies pay out.

8. The primary goal of a ……………..analysis is to identify and assign all significant factors that could positively or negatively impact success to a business.

9. You should try to make sure that you have………….. any time you are doing something that may be very risky.

10. ……………….. is not an innate skill; rather it is a learned set of skills that can be developed at all levels.

11. I invest in ……………..and I've got some in France Telecom recently.

12. Holders of ……………exercise control by electing a board of directors and voting on corporate policy.

13. The performance of a ……………is heavily influenced by the price of the underlying common stock.

14. The disadvantage of …………..is that, customers may leave the brand once prices begin to rise to levels more in line with competitors.

15. The new branch office relied on a regular cash ……………from their parent corporation in order to handle setting up a new location.

16. It is always important to make your payments on time and stay up to date to get rid of your………….. as quick as possible.

17. The ……………..of the corporation must include their yearly dividends as income when they file their taxes at the end of the year.

18. Police officers, postal workers, city employees, and many other people who hold government positions are all part of a typical…………………...

19. Many corporate and government…………… are publicly traded on exchanges, while others are traded only over-the-counter (OTC).

20. …………….payments must be approved by the board of directors.

141. Limited Liability Company (LLC)

Meaning:

A limited liability company (LLC) is a corporate structure whereby the members of the company cannot be held personally liable for the company's debts or liabilities.

Example:

You may want to set yourself up as a limited liability company so that you do not have too much of a burden on you.

Now look it up to understand more, and then make your sentences.

1. _____.
2. _____.
3. _____.

142. Research and Development (R&D)

Meaning:

Research and Development is the process of combining both basic and applied research, and aimed at discovering solutions to problems or creating new products.

Example:

It is important for an organization to always be strong in research and development so that it can come up with new innovative products.

Now look it up to understand more, and then make your sentences.

1. _____.
2. _____.
3. _____.

143. GROSS INCOME

Meaning:
Gross income is the total revenue of a business or individual in an accounting period before deduction of all expenses, allowances, depreciation, or other adjustments.

Example:
The gross income of the company was far higher than its operating income because of high costs for research and development.
Note: Net income is the total revenue in an accounting period **after** deduction of all expenses, allowances, depreciation, or other adjustments during the same period

Now look it up to understand more, and then make your sentences.

1. _____.
2. _____.
3. _____.

144. MARKET SEGMENTATION

Meaning:
The process of defining and subdividing a large homogenous market into clearly identifiable segments having similar needs, wants, or demand characteristics.

Examples:
Market segmentation is based on consumers and allows companies to adjust their sales program to the consumers' needs.

Now look it up to understand more, and then make your sentences.

1. _____.
2. _____.
3. _____.

145. SUPPLY CHAIN MANAGEMENT (SCM)

Meaning:
This is the Management of material and information flow in a supply chain to provide the highest degree of customer satisfaction at the lowest possible cost. Supply chain management requires the commitment of supply chain partners to work closely to coordinate order generation, order taking, and order fulfilment. They thereby create an extended enterprise spreading far beyond the producer's location.

Example:
I was analyzing the organization structure and realized there was a deficiency in the supply chain management because we were having trouble fulfilling our obligations.

Now look it up to understand more, and then make your sentences.

1. _____.
2. _____.
3. _____.

146. LAUNCH A PRODUCT

Meaning
This is the process of introducing a new product or service into the marketplace.

Example:
Manufacturers do numerous market researches before they decide to launch a new product.

Now look it up to understand more, and then make your sentences.

1. _____.
2. _____.
3. _____.

147. OFFEROR/ BIDDER

Meaning:
When a firm makes an official bid to take over a target company, a legal offer is created. The firm making the offer becomes an offeror, while the target becomes the offeree.

Example:
If a target firm accepts an offer, the offeror has an obligation to complete the transaction.

Now look it up to understand more, and then make your sentences.

1. _____.

2. _____.

3. _____.

148. LINE OF CREDIT (LOC)

Meaning:
A line of credit (LOC) is an arrangement between a financial institution, usually a bank, and a customer that establishes a maximum loan balance that the bank will permit the borrower to maintain. The borrower can draw down on the line of credit at any time, as long as he or she does not exceed the maximum set in the agreement.

Example:
You may be able to get a line of credit from your supplier if you have done a lot of business with them in the past.

Now look it up to understand more, and then make your sentences.

1. _____.

2. _____.

3. _____.

149. AUDITOR

Meaning

An auditor is an individual who inspects and verifies the accuracy of a company's operational and/or financial records. Public companies are required to use a public accounting firm for the conduct of an audit of their financial statements.

Example:

Many outsourcing companies recommend their auditors to control finances of other companies.

Now look it up to understand more, and then make your sentences.

1. _____.
2. _____.
3. _____.

150. ORGANIZATIONAL STRUCTURE

Meaning:

This is typically hierarchical arrangement of lines of authority, communications, rights and duties of an organization. Organizational structure determines how the roles, power and responsibilities are assigned, controlled, and coordinated, and how information flows between the different levels of management.

Example:

Having a good organizational structure will lead to much better decisions by a business for its long term investment goals.

Now look it up to understand more, and then make your sentences.

1. _____.
2. _____.
3. _____.

Treasure box 10: Watch and Listen to Business-related Media

> Watching business-themed television shows is an easy way to have fun while still practicing your business English. Remember to pause and re-watch when you don't understand a phrase or conversation. It's also helpful to turn on the English subtitles while you watch. "Shark Tank" is a very good example.

151. Mission statement

Meaning:
A written declaration of an organization's core purpose and focus that normally remains unchanged over time.

Example:
The mission statement of the business was very clear and important to all employees and they will benefit from the direction of the company moving forward.

Now look it up to understand more, and then make your sentences.

1. _____.

2. _____.

3. _____.

152. DOWNTURN

Meaning:
This is a downward shift in an economic cycle, such as from expansion or steady-state to recession. A stock market is in downturn when it changes from a **bull market** to a **bear market**. The opposite is **upturn**.

Example:
When companies have rivals that offer a better product at the same or better price, they often experience a downturn in their stock market profile.

Now look it up to understand more, and then make your sentences.

1. _____.
2. _____.
3. _____.

153. BULL MARKET

Meaning:
Securities or commodities market in which prices are rising, bulls are trading in high volumes, investment interest is high, and the public views the economy as strong and getting stronger.

Example:
When someone invests in the bull market they are taking risks that could either make them or break them.

Now look it up to understand more, and then make your sentences.

1. _____.
2. _____.
3. _____.

154: BEAR MARKET

Meaning:
Period in which prices of securities or commodities fall by 20 percent or more. During such periods (1) investment interest is generally limited, (2) concerns about the state of the economy abound, and (3) dealers or speculators are more inclined in selling their investment portfolios than to increase their risk by holding.

Example:
I wish I had sold the stock that I had in the company because it suddenly dropped considerably when most stocks in that industry fell during a time of bear market.

Now look it up to understand more, and then make your sentences.

1. _____.
2. _____.
3. _____.

155. INFRINGEMENT

Meaning:
Infringement is a violation of the terms of an agreement, encroachment, trespass, or disregard of others' rights, such as invasion of an exclusive right of intellectual property.

Example:
Sometimes another company will pull some form of unnecessary infringement on you and it is up to youwhether to take legal action or not.

Now look it up to understand more, and then make your sentences.

1. _____.
2. _____.
3. _____.

156. KAIZEN

Meaning:
Japanese term for a gradual approach to ever higher standards in quality enhancement and waste reduction, through small but continual improvements involving everyone from the chief executive to the lowest level workers.

Example:
I thought the company must have taken a kaizen approach because they were holding themselves to incredible standards and evolving in a positive fashion

Now look it up to understand more, and then make your sentences.

1. _____.
2. _____.
3. _____.

157. PRO FORMA INVOICE

Meaning:
An abridged or estimated invoice sent by a seller to a buyer in advance of a shipment or delivery of goods. It notes the kind and quantity of goods, their value, and other important information such as weight and transportation charges. Pro forma invoices are commonly used as preliminary invoices with a quotation, or for customs purposes in importation. They differ from a normal invoice in not being a demand or request for payment.

Example:
You should always make sure that any pro forma invoice fully and accurately breaks down everything that needs to be known.

Now look it up to understand more, and then make your sentences.

1. _____.
2. _____.
3. _____.

158. LETTER OF CREDITS

Meaning:
A written commitment to pay, by a buyer's or importer's bank called the issuing bank to the seller's or exporter's bank called, the accepting bank, negotiating bank, or paying bank.

Example:
Whenever I went to buy new equipment for the company I was given a letter of credit instead of cash.

Now look it up to understand more, and then make your sentences.

1. _____.
2. _____.
3. _____.

159. RECONCILIATION

Meaning:
Item by item examination of two related sets of figures obtained from different sources. Most commonly, this term is applied to bank reconciliation.

Example:
I noticed my online statement total did not match the statement total I received in the mail, so I would have to do some reconciliation to find out why they differ.

Now look it up to understand more, and then make your sentences.

1. _____.
2. _____.
3. _____.

160. FINANCIAL MANAGEMENT

Meaning:
Financial management is the planning, directing, monitoring, organizing, and controlling of the monetary resources of an organization.

Example:
You need to be great at financial management if you want to build up your equity and be able to use it to your advantage.

Now look it up to understand more, and then make your sentences.

. _____.

2. _____.

3. _____.

REVIEW QUIZ

1. Many outsourcing companies recommend their ....to control finances of other companies.

2. It is important for an organization to always be strong in ....
so that it can come up with new innovative products.

3. Manufacturers do numerous market researches before they decide to...................... a new product.

4. Whenever I went to buy new equipment for the company I was given a letter of ....instead of cash.

5. The ....of the company was far higher than its operating income because of high costs for research and development.

6. You should always make sure that any.............. invoice fully and accurately breaks down everything that needs to be known.

7. I was analyzing the organization structure and realized there was a deficiency in the supply chain........ because we were having trouble fulfilling our obligations.

8. If a target firm accepts an offer, the ....has an obligation to complete the transaction.

9. I thought the company must have taken a ....approach because they were holding themselves to incredible standards and evolving in a positive fashion

10. You may be able to get a.............. of credit from your supplier if you have done a lot of business with them in the past.

11. Having a good organizational.............. will lead to much better decisions by a business for its long term investment goals.

12. The mission.................... of the business was very clear and important to all employees and they will benefit from the direction of the company moving forward.

13. When someone invests in the ....market they are taking risks that could either make them or break them.

14. Market ....is based on consumers and allows companies to adjust their sales program to the consumers' needs.

15. You may want to set yourself up as a limited liability company so that you do not have too much of a............ on you.

16. I wish I had sold the stock that I had in the company because it suddenly dropped considerably when most stocks in that industry fell during a time of..................... market.

17. You need to be great at financial ....if you want to build up your equity and be able to use it to your advantage.

18. When companies have rivals that offer a better product at the same or better price, they often experience a ....in their stock market profile.

19. Sometimes another company will pull some form of unnecessary .... on you and it is up to you whether to take legal action or not.

20. I noticed my online statement total did not match the statement total I received in the mail, so I would have to do some ....to find out why they differ.

161. SELF-EFFICACY

Meaning:
This term means a person's belief about his or her ability and capacity to accomplish a task or to deal with the challenges of life.

Example:
People who read personal development books usually have a high level of self-efficacy and are able to take care of themselves, their business or carrier and / or thrive in our modern day society.

Now look it up to understand more, and then make your sentences.

1. _____.
2. _____.
3. _____.

162. SELF-ACTUALIZATION

Meaning:
It is the motivation to realize one's own maximum potential and possibilities. It is considered to be the master motive or the only real motive, all other motives being its various forms.

Example:
Having lost his first, second and third races, the sprinter used this as the self-actualization to improve and do the best he could.

Now look it up to understand more, and then make your sentences.

1. _____.
2. _____.
3. _____.

163. SUCCESS

Meaning:
Success can mean the completion of an objective or reaching a goal. Success can be expanded to encompass an entire project or be restricted to a single component of a project or task. It can be achieved within the workplace, or in an individual's personal life.

Example:
The fundraising campaign was a huge success, exceeding its original goal by over 30% in just the first five days.

Now look it up to understand more, and then make your sentences.

1. _____.
2. _____.
3. _____.

164. ASSESSMENT

Meaning:
Procedure used to evaluate a situation or person or determine the value of a property, or the income of a person or entity.

Example:
The government employee sent his assessment regarding the value of the land to his boss who would decide if it was fiscally sound to purchase the property.

Now look it up to understand more, and then make your sentences.

1. _____.
2. _____.
3. _____.

165. CONSENSUS

Meaning:
Consensus is the Middle ground in decision making, between total assent and total disagreement. Consensus depends on participants having shared values and goals, and on having broad agreement on specific issues and overall direction.

Example:
There was a consensus among the group, but one of them couldnot shake off the feeling that they were overlooking something really important.

Now look it up to understand more, and then make your sentences.

1. _____.

2. _____.

3. _____.

TREASURE BOX 11: NEED VS. SUCCESS

Look at this Maslow's hierarchy of needs diagram.

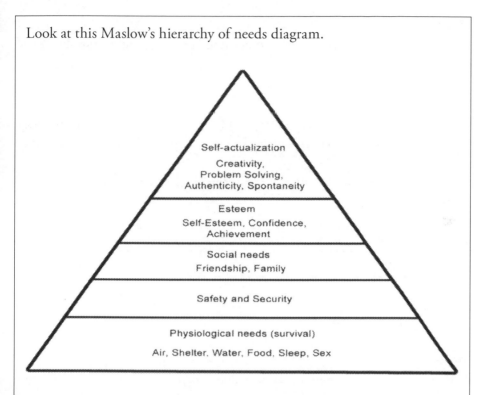

In Maslow's hierarchy of needs, the need for self-actualization is the final need that manifests when lower level needs have been satisfied.

What is your need? Your need is very important and will determine your success not only in speaking English Language fluently, but also in your career and life.

166. PARAMETER

Meaning:
A rule or limit that controls what something is or how something should be done.

Example:
The most important parameter of the user base was age, as that was most likely to correlate to the users purchasing decisions, as opposed to gender or location.

Now look it up to understand more, and then make your sentences.

1. _____.
2. _____.
3. _____.

167. FORECLOSURE

Meaning:
A situation in which a homeowner is unable to make full principal and interest payments on his/her mortgage, which allows the lender to seize the property, evict the homeowner and sell the home, as stipulated in the mortgage contract.

Example:
My friend's home, along with many other people's went into foreclosure because he could not make the payments.

Now look it up to understand more, and then make your sentences.

1. _____.
2. _____.
3. _____.

168. SYNERGY

Meaning:
The increased effectiveness that results when two or more people or businesses work together as a team.

Example:
A synergy has developed among the different groups working on this project.

Now look it up to understand more, and then make your sentences.

1. _____.
2. _____.
3. _____.

169. IMPERATIVE

Meaning:
Imperative means absolutely important or necessary.

Example:
It is imperative that we continue to move with speed to make housing more affordable.

Now look it up to understand more, and then make your sentences.

1. _____.
2. _____.
3. _____.

170. DEDUCTIBLE

Meaning:
A certain cost that can be subtracted from an amount of money.

Example:
The trip was deductible as a business expense.

Now look it up to understand more, and then make your sentences.

1. _____.
2. _____.
3. _____.

171. PREMISES

Meaning:
1. A building or facility, including the fenced or walled (or demarcated or segregated) space surrounding it.
2. Issues or matters raised or referred to in the earlier part of an argument or document.

Examples:
1. The company is relocating to new premises.
2. The youth delivered his essay to his teacher. However after reading the essay, the teacher gave the youth a bad score because of his weak premises.

Now look it up to understand more, and then make your sentences.

1. _____.
2. _____.
3. _____.

172. ADAPTATION

Meaning:
Edited or revised version of a work aimed at serving a specific purpose.

Example:
Since the play was over 50 years old, I decided to create a brand new adaptation in which the characters live in a modern society.

Now look it up to understand more, and then make your sentences.

1. _____.
2. _____.
3. _____.

173. ECONOMIC RECESSION

Meaning:
Period of general economic decline, defined usually as a contraction in the GDP for six months (two consecutive quarters) or longer. Marked by high unemployment, stagnant wages, and fall in retail sales.

Example:
The account broker lost most of his money during the recession, but made it all back in the few years that followed.

Now look it up to understand more, and then make your sentences.

1. _____.
2. _____.
3. _____.

174. GROSS DOMESTIC PRODUCT (GDP)

Meaning:

The value of a country's overall output of goods and services (typically during one fiscal year) at market prices, excluding net income from abroad.

Gross Domestic Product (GDP) can be estimated in three ways which, in theory, should yield identical figures. They are

(1) Expenditure basis: how much money was spent,

(2) Output basis: how many goods and services were sold, and

(3) Income basis: how much income (profit) was earned.

These estimates, published quarterly, are constantly revised to approach greater accuracy.

Example:

The finance ministers were under a lot of pressure to improve the country's economic situation and, for that reason, they focused on their nation's gross domestic product and how they could improve it.

Now look it up to understand more, and then make your sentences.

1. _____.

2. _____.

3. _____.

175. GROSS NATIONAL PRODUCT (GNP)

Meaning:
This is the GDP of a country to which income from abroad remittances of nationals living outside and income from foreign subsidiaries of local firms has been added.

Example:
When I think of analyzing governments and countries from an economic perspective I prefer to learn about the country's gross national product.

Now look it up to understand more, and then make your sentences.

1. _____.
2. _____.
3. _____.

176. MIXED ECONOMY

Meaning:
This is an economic system in which both the private enterprise and a degree of state monopoly (usually in public services, defense, infrastructure, and basic industries) coexist. All modern economies are mixed where the means of production are shared between the private and public sectors. It is also called dual economy.

Example:
In the U.S.A the market would be considered a mixed economy unlike most European countries that favor state-owned resources.

Now look it up to understand more, and then make your sentences.

1. _____.
2. _____.
3. _____.

177. ECONOMIC DEPRESSION

Meaning:
Lowest point in an economic cycle characterized by (1) reduced purchasing power, (2) mass unemployment, (3) excess of supply over demand, (4) falling prices, or prices rising slower than usual, (5) falling wages, or wages rising slower than usual, and (6) general lack of confidence in the future. Also called a **slump**, a depression of economy causes a drop in all economic activity.

Example:
During the economic depression, the stock market plummeted, many businesses were forced to close their doors, and millions of people lost their jobs.

Now look it up to understand more, and then make your sentences.

1. _____.
2. _____.
3. _____.

178. BANKRUPTCY

Legal procedure for liquidating a business (or property owned by an individual) which cannot fully pay its debts out of its current assets.

Example:
If you get yourself into so much debt that you don't think there is any way out your last resort may be to declare bankruptcy.

Now look it up to understand more, and then make your sentences.

1. _____.
2. _____.
3. _____.

179. SERENDIPITY

Meaning:
It is the good luck in making unexpected and fortunate discoveries

Example:
If you find good things without looking for them, serendipity has brought them to you.

Now look it up to understand more, and then make your sentences.

1. _____.
2. _____.
3. _____.

180. HELICOPTER DROP

Meaning:
Helicopter drop is an unconventional tool of monetary policy that involves printing large sums of money and distributing it to the public in order to stimulate the economy.

Example:
The objective of Helicopter drop is largely to jumpstart the economy during deflationary periods.

Now look it up to understand more, and then make your sentences.

1. _____.
2. _____.
3. _____.

REVIEW QUIZ

1. When I think of analyzing governments and countries from an economic perspective I prefer to learn about the country's ....national product.

2. In the U.S.A the market would be considered a............ economy unlike most European countries that favor state-owned resources.

3. The company is relocating to new....................

4. During the economic ....the stock market plummeted, many businesses were forced to close their doors, and millions of people lost their jobs.

5. People who read personal development books usually have a high level of ....and are able to take care of themselves, their business or carrier and /or thrive in our modern day society.

6. A synergy has ....among the different groups working on this project.

7. There was a ....among the group, but one of them could not shake off the feeling that they were overlooking something really important.

8. My friend's home, along with many other people's went into ....because he could not make the payments.

9. It is................. that we continue to move with speed to make housing more affordable.

10. If you get yourself into so much debt that you don't think there is any way out your last resort may be to declare ....

11. Since the play was over 50 years old, I decided to create a brand new ....in which the characters live in a modern society.

12. The trip was...................... as a business expense.

13. The most important ....of the user base was age, as that was most likely to correlate to the users purchasing decisions, as opposed to gender or location.

14. The account broker lost most of his money during the ....but made it all back in the few years that followed.

15. The finance ministers were under a lot of pressure to improve the country's economic situation and, for that reason, they focused on their nation's................ domestic product and how they could improve it.

16. If you find good things without looking for them, ...has brought them to you.

17. The objective of ....drop is largely to jumpstart the economy during deflationary periods.

18. Having lost his first, second and third races, the sprinter used this as the self................... to improve and do the best he could.

19. The fundraising campaign was a huge.............., exceeding its original goal by over 30% in just the first five days.

20. The government employee sent his................ regarding the value of the land to his boss who would decide if it was fiscally sound to purchase the property.

Treasure box 12: Successful vs. Unsuccessful people

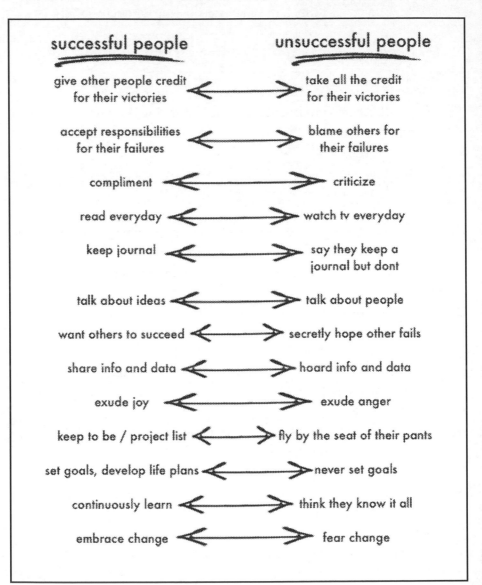

successful people	unsuccessful people
give other people credit for their victories	take all the credit for their victories
accept responsibilities for their failures	blame others for their failures
compliment	criticize
read everyday	watch tv everyday
keep journal	say they keep a journal but dont
talk about ideas	talk about people
want others to succeed	secretly hope other fails
share info and data	hoard info and data
exude joy	exude anger
keep to be / project list	fly by the seat of their pants
set goals, develop life plans	never set goals
continuously learn	think they know it all
embrace change	fear change

181. ANOMALY

Meaning:
Anomaly is the deviation from the norm; something unusual.

Example:
Bob searched the data for anomalies that would indicate that there was an error with the system.

Now look it up to understand more, and then make your sentences.

1. _____.
2. _____.
3. _____.

182. PERVASIVE

Meaning:
Pervasive is used for something or concept that is widespread, literally or figuratively existing in or spreading through every part of something or everywhere.

Example:
Agile software development has become pervasive in the technology industry.

Now look it up to understand more, and then make your sentences.

1. _____.
2. _____.
3. _____.

183. INFORMATION REVOLUTION

Meaning:
Development of technologies (such as computers, digital communication, microchips) in the second half of the 20th century that has led to dramatic reduction in the cost of obtaining, processing, storing, and transmitting information in all forms (text, graphics, audio, video).

Example:
The information revolution has enabled many people to actualize their dreams and satisfy their curiosity by learning nearly any concept.

Now look it up to understand more, and then make your sentences.

1. _____.
2. _____.
3. _____.

184. HIATUS

Meaning:
Hiatus is a temporary pause or break. The term is commonly used to designate a break in continuous airing of a television show, such as the break between seasons, or a break in a person's employment or artiste's history.

Example:
The band is making an album again after a five-year hiatus.

Now look it up to understand more, and then make your sentences.

1. _____.
2. _____.
3. _____.

185. COMMAND ECONOMY

Meaning:
An economy in which market mechanisms are replaced by a centralized state authority which coordinates all economic activity through commands, directives and regulations for the purpose of achieving broader socio-economic and political objectives.

Example:
The United States is a mix economy, and in the past has politically battled centralized governments that have used a command economy instead of a capitalist or free market one.

Now look it up to understand more, and then make your sentences.

1. _____.
2. _____.
3. _____.

186. AMBIGUOUS

Meaning:
Something that is unclear or uncertain. An ambiguous phrase is one that is not easy to understand, and often could be interpreted different ways. Something ambiguous can occasionally be deceptive, either intentionally or unintentionally, because the interpreter isn't able to figure out the actual meaning.

Example:
The word "biweekly" is ambiguous, because it can mean either happening every two weeks or happening twice a week.

Now look it up to understand more, and then make your sentences.

1. _____.
2. _____.
3. _____.

187. ACQUISITION

Meaning:
This is taking control or possession of an asset or of records or of a firm by purchasing 51 percent (or more) of its shares.

Example:
Looking to expand their business, the mobile provider made an acquisition of a company whose primary service is cable television.

Now look it up to understand more, and then make your sentences.

1. _____.
2. _____.
3. _____.

188. STEREOTYPE

Meaning:
Erroneous, relatively fixed, simplistic, and mostly negative generalization (based commonly on bigotry, ignorance, and prejudice) held to be true about certain individuals or groups.

Example:
Shawn was disappointed with his classmates and their attitude towards him, as they believed he would not be a good academic partner due to stereotypes about his race.

Now look it up to understand more, and then make your sentences.

1. _____.
2. _____.
3. _____.

189. PARADIGM

Meaning:
This term means an intellectual perception or view, accepted by an individual or a society as a clear example, model, or pattern of how things work in the world.

Example:
As technological innovation continues, there is a paradigm shift as we change the way we think and act.

Now look it up to understand more, and then make your sentences.

1. _____.
2. _____.
3. _____.

190. AUTONOMY

Meaning:
This is a degree or level of freedom and discretion allowed to an employee over his or her job.

Example:
Some employees resent frequent interference and micromanagement by their superiors, preferring autonomy in their work, while others fail to thrive without constant supervision.

Now look it up to understand more, and then make your sentences.

1. _____.
2. _____.
3. _____.

191. PER DIEM

Meaning:

Per Diem is a phrase usually used to describe something you get on a daily basis. If you are getting paid per diem, you are getting paid a certain wage for the day.

Example:

If you're lucky enough to get a per diem allowance at your job, you probably have quite a good job.

Now look it up to understand more, and then make your sentences.

1. _____.

2. _____.

3. _____.

192. MINIMUM WAGE

Meaning:

Lowest hourly rate an employer can pay an employee.

Example:

In some countries (such as the US) the minimum wage is set by a statute while in others (such as the UK) it is set by the wage council of each industry.

Now look it up to understand more, and then make your sentences.

1. _____.

2. _____.

3. _____.

193. ECONOMIES OF SCALE

Meaning:
The reduction in long-run average and marginal costs arising from an increase in size of an operating unit (a factory or plant).

Example:
As the company grew, it continued to drop its prices as economies of scale drove down manufacturing costs.

Now look it up to understand more, and then make your sentences.

1. _____.
2. _____.
3. _____.

194. AVERAGE COST

Meaning:
Production cost per unit of output, computed by dividing the total of fixed costs and variable costs by the number of total units produced (total output). (Fixed costs + Variable costs) ÷ Total output

Example:
By lowering the average cost of our product we will be able to still charge the same price and make more money on each sale, thus increasing our profit margins while not risking losing customers.

Now look it up to understand more, and then make your sentences.

1. _____.
2. _____.
3. _____.

195. MARGINAL COST

Meaning:
The increase or decrease in the total cost of a production run for making one additional unit of an item. It is calculated as
MC = Change in total cost (TC) / Change in quantity (Q).

Example:
The marginal cost of adding additional sticks of RAM in the new Dell laptops, far outweighs the usefulness that the consumer will see in the performance.

Now look it up to understand more, and then make your sentences.

1. _____.
2. _____.
3. _____.

REASSURE BOX 13: TRANSFER OF KNOWLEDGE

Because learning involves transfer from previous experiences, one's existing knowledge can also make it difficult to learn new information. Sometimes new information will seem incomprehensible, but this feeling of confusion can at least let you identify the existence of a problem and may motivate you.

196. PRINCIPAL

Meaning:
A major party in a business transaction or Capital as distinct from the income (interest) derived from it.

Example:
The principal beneficiary of the will received two-thirds of the man's estate, while the other members of the family divided up the remaining third.

Now look it up to understand more, and then make your sentences.

1. _____.
2. _____.
3. _____.

197. DIPLOMACY

Meaning:
It is an instrument by which a state (or, by extension, an organization or individual) attempts to achieve its aims, in relation to those of others, through dialogue and negotiation.

Example:
When working in a position alongside elected officials and the public, one must use diplomacy to get desired results while keeping both groups satisfied.

Now look it up to understand more, and then make your sentences.

1. _____.
2. _____.
3. _____.

198. ATTRITION

Meanings:
1. The unpredictable and uncontrollable, but normal, reduction of work force due to resignations, retirement, sickness, or death.
2. Loss of a material or resource due to obsolescence or spoilage.

Example
If your company has high attrition, you will be forced to continuously advertise, interview and hire new employees to take the place of those employees who have left.

Now look it up to understand more, and then make your sentences.

1. _____.
2. _____.
3. _____.

199. NEPOTISM

Meaning:
Practice of appointing relatives and friends in one's organization to positions for which outsiders might be better qualified.

Example:
Despite its negative connotations, nepotism (if applied sensibly) is an important and positive practice in the startup and formative years of a firm where complete trust and willingness to work hard (for little or no immediate reward) are critical for its survival.

Now look it up to understand more, and then make your sentences.

1. _____.
2. _____.
3. _____.

200. SIN STOCK

Meaning:
Also known as "sinful stocks" is a stock of a company directly associated with activities widely considered to be illegal, unethical or immoral. Sin stock sectors include alcohol, tobacco, gambling, sex-related industries, weapons manufacturers and the military.

Example:
Sinful stocks are the polar opposite of ethical investing and socially responsible investing, whose proponents emphasize investments that benefit society.

Now look it up to understand more, and then make your sentences.

1. _____.

2. _____.

3. _____.

REVIEW QUIZ

1. The band is making an album again after a five-year...........

2. Looking to expand their business, the mobile provider made an ....of a company whose primary service is cable television.

3. Bob searched the data for ....that would indicate that there was an error with the system.

4. The word "biweekly" is..............., because it can mean either happening every two weeks or happening twice a week.

5. By lowering the ....cost of our product we will be able to still charge the same price and make more money on each sale, thus increasing our profit margins while not risking losing customers

6. Agile software developments has become ....in the technology industry.

7. Some employees resent frequent interference and micro-management by their superiors, preferring ....in their work, while others fail to thrive without constant supervision.

8. The United States is a mix economy, and in the past has politically battled centralized governments that have used a ....economy instead of a capitalist or free market one.

9. The information ....has enabled many people to actualize their dreams and satisfy their curiosity by learning nearly any concept.

10. The................... beneficiary of the will received two-thirds of the man's estate, while the other members of the family divided up the remaining third.

11. Shawn was disappointed with his classmates and their attitude towards him, as they believed he would not be a good academic partner due to ....about his race.

12. In some countries (such as the US) the minimum ....is set by a statute while in others (such as the UK) it is set by the wage council of each industry.

13. If you're lucky enough to get a per ....allowance at your job, you probably have quite a good job.

14. ....stocks are the polar opposite of ethical investing and socially responsible investing, whose proponents emphasize investments that benefit society.

15. When working in a position alongside elected officials and the public, one must use ....to get desired results while keeping both groups satisfied.

16. As the company grew, it continued to drop its prices as economies of............. drove down manufacturing costs.

17. As technological innovation continues, there is a ....shift as we change the way we think and act.

18. The ....cost of adding additional sticks of RAM in the new Dell laptops, far outweighs the usefulness that the consumer will see in the performance.

19. If your company has high................. you will be forced to continuously advertise, interview and hire new employees to take the place of those employees who have left.

20. Despite its negative connotations,............. is an important and positive practice in the startup and formative years of a firm.

201. LEVERAGE

Meaning:
Leverage is the advantageous condition of having a relatively small amount of cost yield a relatively high level of returns.

Example:
The company can leverage its assets to request better terms of agreement for building expansion loan, for example smaller down payments, or lower interest rates.

Now look it up to understand more, and then make your sentences.

1. _____.
2. _____.
3. _____.

202. INTEGRATION

Meanings:
1. General: process of attaining close and seamless coordination between several departments, groups, organizations, systems, etc.
2. Companies: merger of two or more firms resulting in a new legal entity.
3. Contracts: amalgamation of two or more agreements into one contract that serves as a full expression of the intent of the contracting parties.

EXAMPLE
The company also allows social network integration, which allows you to easily share your job posting across Twitter, Facebook, etc.

Now look it up to understand more, and then make your sentences.

1. _____.
2. _____.
3. _____.

203. CORPORATE SOCIAL RESPONSIBILITY

Meaning:
This is a company's sense of responsibility toward the community and environment (both ecological and social) in which it operates.

Example:
Although most companies nowadays practice some form of Corporate Social Responsibility, some companies have made it their primary focus.

Now look it up to understand more, and then make your sentences.

1. _____.
2. _____.
3. _____.

204. WHITE PAPER

Meaning:
A concise report or marketing tool that informs readers about a complex issue, often used to convey an organization's philosophy and persuade potential customers.

Example:
I have laid out the proposals in the white paper that we had spoken about previously during our consultation and would like you to review before it is submitted.

Now look it up to understand more, and then make your sentences.

1. _____.
2. _____.
3. _____.

205. DERIVATIVE

Meaning:
In finance it means contract to buy or sell an asset or exchange cash, based on a specified condition, event, occurrence, or another contract.

Example:
The derivative of my financial stock gains last week was from the purchases I made in oil and technology stocks the previous week.

Now look it up to understand more, and then make your sentences.

1. _____.
2. _____.
3. _____.

206. PORTFOLIO

Meaning:
Pool of investments, collection of samples of an artist or other creative person, or group of complementary or supplementary products marketed together.

Example:
Melissa worked hard on finishing new paintings and drawings for her portfolio before her interview at the prestigious art school in the city.

Now look it up to understand more, and then make your sentences.

1. _____.
2. _____.
3. _____.

207. FOREIGN POLICY

Meaning:
Plan of action adopted by one nation in regards to its diplomatic dealings with other countries. Foreign policies are established as a systematic way to deal with issues that may arise with other countries.

Example:
The United States has a different foreign policy for almost every country, and the policies can vary based on trade agreements in addition to many other conditions.

Now look it up to understand more, and then make your sentences.

1. _____.
2. _____.
3. _____.

208: MIDDLE CLASS

Meaning:
This is the Social class usually comprising of white-collar (non-manual) workers, lower-level managers, and small business owners, often constituting about one-third of the employed population of a country.

Example:
The most diverse of all the social classes in America is perhaps the middle class due to the vast range of incomes and occupations that it encompasses.

Now look it up to understand more, and then make your sentences.

1. _____.
2. _____.
3. _____.

209. ECONOMIC CRISIS

Meaning:
A situation in which the economy of a country experiences a sudden downturn brought on by a financial crisis.

Example:
The news of the economic crisis had everyone working the stock market in a panic to sell their stocks before the downfall.

Now look it up to understand more, and then make your sentences.

1. _____.
2. _____.
3. _____.

210 BILLS OF LADING (B/L)

Meaning:
A document issued by a carrier, or its agent, to the shipper as a contract of carriage of goods. It is also a receipt for cargo accepted for transportation, and must be presented for taking delivery at the destination.

Example:
The bill of lading needs to be signed for and reviewed for accuracy, and a copy of it needs to be sent to the receiving manager and finance in order to satisfy record keeping procedures.

Now look it up to understand more, and then make your sentences.

1. _____.
2. _____.
3. _____.

TREASURE BOX 14: INTERESTED IN FREIGHT BUSINESS?

Among other items of information, a bill of lading contains (1) consignor's and consignee's name, (2) names of the ports of departure and destination, (3) name of the vessel, (4) dates of departure and arrival, (5) itemized list of goods being transported with number of packages and kind of packaging, (6) marks and numbers on the packages, (7) weight and/or volume of the cargo, (8) freight rate and amount.

211. BARTER

Meaning:
Trading in which goods or services are exchanged without the use of cash. Resorted-to usually in times of high inflation or tight money, barter is now a common form of trading where items ranging from manufacturing capacity to steel and paper are bartered across international borders on a daily basis.

Example:
Before societies used money to pay for goods and services they used the barter system and in the end everyone ended up with something they needed.

Now look it up to understand more, and then make your sentences.

1. _____.

2. _____.

3. _____.

212. BALANCE OF TRADE (BOT)

Meaning:
Largest component of a country's current account in its balance of payments (BOP) accounts, it shows the difference between export earnings and import expenditure. It is called **'favorable'** when the amount realized from physical (or tangible or visible) exports is more than the amount spent on physical imports, otherwise called **'unfavorable.'** Also called trade balance.

Example:
It is important that a country has a good record of their imports and exports to get the right answer for what is their balance of trade.

Now look it up to understand more, and then make your sentences.

1. _____.
2. _____.
3. _____.

213. FISCAL POLICY

Meaning:
Government's revenue (taxation) and spending policy designed to (1) counter economic cycles in order to achieve lower unemployment, (2) achieve low or no inflation, and (3) achieve sustained but controllable economic growth.

Example:
Some constituents in our country disagree with our president's fiscal policy, and they say that he spends too much of their money.

Now look it up to understand more, and then make your sentences.

1. _____.
2. _____.
3. _____.

214. ABATEMENT

Meaning:

Abatement may mean the elimination or reduction of polluting or hazardous substances (such as asbestos) by either removing them completely or lessening their effect through better waste management.

Example:

When removing the siding from my old house I used abatement in choosing the proper disposal techniques for the asbestos materials.

Now look it up to understand more, and then make your sentences.

1. _____.

2. _____.

3. _____.

215. COMPETITION

Meaning:

Competition is the Rivalry in which every seller tries to get what other sellers are seeking at the same time: sales, profit, and market share by offering the best practicable combination of price, quality, and service.

Example:

Where the market information flows freely, competition plays a regulatory function in balancing demand and supply.

Now look it up to understand more, and then make your sentences.

1. _____.

2. _____.

3. _____.

216. NEGOTIATION

Meaning:
Bargaining process between two or more parties each with its own aims, needs, and viewpoints seeking to discover a common ground and reach an agreement to settle a matter of mutual concern or resolve a conflict.

Example:
It is not always important to win or be right because sometimes relationships are more important than the argument and a negotiation can save a relationship.

Now look it up to understand more, and then make your sentences.

1. _____.
2. _____.
3. _____.

217. BIT COIN

Meaning:
Created in 2009, is a digital currency that is completely decentralized. It facilitates payments by using peer-to-peer technology and can be used on the internet or in brick and mortar stores.

Example:
Bit Coin is considered a type of crypto-currency because it uses cryptography for security, making it extremely difficult to counterfeit.

Now look it up to understand more, and then make your sentences.

1. _____.
2. _____.
3. _____.

218. ACCOUNTABILITY

Meaning:

The obligation of an individual or organization to account for its activities, accept responsibility for them, and to disclose the results in a transparent manner.

Example:

The billing department was experiencing worker performance issues so they developed new workplace procedures, to track worker performance and accountability to ones work.

Now look it up to understand more, and then make your sentences.

1. _____.
2. _____.
3. _____.

219. VENDOR

Meaning:

A person who sells something, especially a property is a vendor.

Example:

I am hungry;I have to go to the hotdog vendor before the next play. Can you pass me my wallet so I can purchase something?.

Now look it up to understand more, and then make your sentences.

1. _____.
2. _____.
3. _____.

220. GANTT CHART

Meaning:
It is a type of bar-chart that shows both the scheduled and completed work over a period. A time-scale is given on the chart's horizontal axis and each activity is shown as a separate horizontal rectangle (bar) whose length is proportional to the time required (or taken) for the activity's completion. In project planning, these charts show start and finish dates, critical and non-critical activities, slack time, and predecessor-successor relationships.

Example:
When giving a presentation a Gantt chart can be a good way to convey all of your information to your audience.

Now look it up to understand more, and then make your sentences.

1. _____.

2. _____.

3. _____.

REVIEW QUIZ

1. The ....of my financial stock gains last week was from the purchases I made in oil and technology stocks the previous week.

2. The news of the economic ....had everyone working the stock market in a panic to sell their stocks before the downfall.

3. The United States has a different foreign policy for almost every country, and the ....can vary based on trade agreements in addition to many other conditions.

4. Where the market information flows freely, ...plays a regulatory function in balancing demand and supply.

5. The most diverse of all the social classes in America is perhaps the ....due to the vast range of incomes and occupations that it encompasses.

6. Melissa worked hard on finishing new paintings and drawings for her........... before her interview at the prestigious art school in the city.

7. The bill of ....needs to be signed for and reviewed for accuracy, and a copy of it needs to be sent to the receiving manager and finance in order to satisfy record keeping procedures.

8. Some constituents in our country disagree with our president's ....policy, and they say that he spends too much of their money.

9. Before societies used money to pay for goods and services they used the ....system and in the end everyone ended up with something they needed.

10. When removing the siding from my old house I used ....in choosing the proper disposal techniques for the asbestos materials.

11. It is not always important to win or be right because sometimes relationships are more important than the argument and a.................. can save a relationship.

12. I am hungry; I have to go to the hotdog ....before the next play. Can you pass me my wallet so I can purchase something?

13. ....is considered a type of crypto-currency because it uses cryptography for security, making it extremely difficult to counterfeit.

14. It is important that a country has a good record of their imports and exports to get the right answer for what is their ....of trade.

15. The billing department was experiencing worker performance issues so they developed new workplace procedures, to track worker performance and ....to ones work.

16. When giving a presentation a ....chart can be a good way to convey all of your information to your audience.

17. The company can............ its assets to request better terms of agreement for building expansion loan, for example smaller down payments, or lower interest rates.

18. They also allow ....network integration, which allows you to easily share your job posting across Twitter, Facebook, and LinkedIn etc.

19. Although most companies nowadays practice some form of Corporate ....Responsibility, some companies have made it their primary focus.

20. I have laid out the proposals in the ....paper that we had spoken about previously during our consultation and would like you to review before it is submitted.

221. INVESTMENT

Meaning:
An investment is an asset or item that is purchased with the hope that it will generate income or appreciate in the future.

Example:
You should always know every little detail about any potential investment so that you can be prepared for anything and everything.

Now look it up to understand more, and then make your sentences.

1. _____.
2. _____.
3. _____.

222. RETURN ON INVESTMENT (ROI)

Meaning:
Return on investment or ROI is the earning power of assets usually measured as a percentage, the ratio return to the capital employed in a company or project. It indicates whether or not a company is using its resources in an efficient manner.

Example:
The return on investment was consistent year after year so we promptly invested more in the company.

Now look it up to understand more, and then make your sentences.

1. _____.
2. _____.
3. _____.

223. PRIVATIZATION

Meaning:
Privatization is the transfer of ownership of property or businesses from a government to a privately owned entity.

Example:
I would suggest privatization as the optimal decision here as the government is inefficient and should not be involved as a rule.

Now look it up to understand more, and then make your sentences.

1. _____.
2. _____.
3. _____.

224. NATIONALIZATION

Meaning:
Nationalization, (the opposite of Privatization) is the takeover of privately owned corporations, industries, and resources by a government with or without compensation.

Example:
The nationalization of the company was unexpected but we prepared for this moment so we simply worked our plan and adapted.

Now look it up to understand more, and then make your sentences.

1. _____.
2. _____.
3. _____.

225. MARKET SHARE

Meaning:

Market share is the percentage of total sales volume in a market captured by a brand, product, or company over a specific period of time.

Example:

We were able to improve our market share by investing heavily in our marketing and advertising as we knew we had a great product.

Now look it up to understand more, and then make your sentences.

1. _____.

2. _____.

3. _____.

TREASURE BOX 15: USE SENTENCE CONNECTORS

Connectors are used to link large groups of words, phrases and sentences. You can also use them to connect paragraphs to give them coherence. Sentence connectors such as; Nevertheless, Likewise, are usually placed at the beginning of a sentence.

226. FEASIBILITY STUDIES

Meaning:
Feasibility studies, also called feasibility analysis is an analysis and evaluation of a proposed project to determine if it is technically feasible within the estimated cost, and will be profitable. Feasibility studies are almost always conducted where large sum of money is at stake.

Example:
Major corporations take advantage of the opportunity to conduct a feasibility study on any new investments they make.

Now look it up to understand more, and then make your sentences.

1. _____.
2. _____.
3. _____.

227. BUSINESS PLAN

Meaning:
Business plan is a set of documents prepared by a firm's management to summarize its operational and financial objectives for the near future (usually one to three years) and to show how they will be achieved. It serves as a blueprint to guide the firm's policies and strategies, and is continually modified as conditions change and new opportunities and/or threats emerge.

Example:
The company published its most recent business plan and distributed it to a group of potential investors and other interested parties.

Now look it up to understand more, and then make your sentences.

1. _____.
2. _____.
3. _____.

228. INVESTOR

Meaning:

An investor is any person who commits capital with the expectation of financial returns. Or whose primary objectives are preservation of the original investment (the principal), a steady income, and capital appreciation.

Example:

It's very common for individuals who are trying to start their own business to look into finding an investor to provide them with startup money.

Now look it up to understand more, and then make your sentences.

1. _____.
2. _____.
3. _____.

229. VENTURE CAPITALIST

Meaning:

A venture capitalist is an investor who either provides capital to startup ventures or supports small companies that wish to expand but do not have access to equities markets.

Example:

Venture capitalists are willing to invest in companies because they can earn a massive return on their investments if these companies are a success.

Now look it up to understand more, and then make your sentences.

1. _____.
2. _____.
3. _____.

230. MULTINATIONAL CORPORATION (MNC)

Meaning:
Multinational Corporation is an enterprise operating in several countries but managed from one (home) country. Generally, any company or group that derives a quarter of its revenue from operations outside of its home country is considered a multinational corporation.

Example:
If you want your product to grow you can turn your business into a multinational corporation to find many new customers.

Now look it up to understand more, and then make your sentences.

1. _____.
2. _____.
3. _____.

231. INITIAL PUBLIC OFFERING - IPO

Meaning:
An initial public offering (IPO) is the first sale of stock by a private company to the public. IPOs are often issued by smaller, younger companies seeking the capital to expand, but can also be done by large privately owned companies looking to become publicly traded.

Example:
If you know of a new company that you think will succeed you may want to take a chance on its initial public offering.

Now look it up to understand more, and then make your sentences.

1. _____.
2. _____.
3. _____.

232. SALES REPRESENTATIVE

Meaning:

Sales representative is a salesperson or agent (whether or not under the direct control of a firm) authorized to solicit business for a firm, and compensated usually through a commission or salary, or a combination of both.

Example:

The salesperson became very successful because of her excellent skills in detailing the benefits of the product she was selling to the client, and could often use that skill to close the sale.

Now look it up to understand more, and then make your sentences.

1. _____.

2. _____.

3. _____.

233. HUMAN RESOURCES

Meaning:

Human resources (Formerly called personnel) is the division of a company that is focused on activities relating to employees. These activities normally include recruiting and hiring of new employees, orientation and training of current employees, employee benefits, and retention.

Example:

When I got my new job, I had to report to the human resources department for new worker orientation and to set up my tax information.

Now look it up to understand more, and then make your sentences.

1. _____.

2. _____.

3. _____.

234. HEADHUNTING

Meaning:
Headhunting is a form of recruitment and selection where the recruiter or headhunter finds the contact details of a specific candidate that has some specific skills and contacts him/her in order to convince him/her to participate in the recruitment process.

Example:
Don't be too excited because you have been called by a headhunter, but your chances for the job are higher than those of some other regular candidates that applied directly.

Now look it up to understand more, and then make your sentences.

1. _____.
2. _____.
3. _____.

235. INSURANCE POLICY

Meaning:
Formal contract-document issued by an insurance company in which an individual or entity receives financial protection or reimbursement against losses from the insurance company.

Example:
Any time you will be taking on a risky venture it is important to take out an insurance policy and protect yourself.

Now look it up to understand more, and then make your sentences.

1. _____.
2. _____.
3. _____.

236. PREMIUM

Meaning:

Premium is the specified amount of payment required periodically by an insurer to provide coverage under a given insurance plan for a defined period of time.

Example:

The amount of insurance premium that is required for insurance coverage depends on a variety of factors.

Now look it up to understand more, and then make your sentences.

1. _____.
2. _____.
3. _____.

237. GOLDILOCKS ECONOMY

Meaning:

This is an economy that sustains moderate economic growth and low inflation, allowing for a market-supportive monetary policy. The economy is thought to be neither too hot nor cold, and allows the markets and wealth generation to be consistent and steady.

Example:

A Goldilocks economy may occur during the recovery and/or growth phases.

Now look it up to understand more, and then make your sentences.

1. _____.
2. _____.
3. _____.

238. EMBARGO

Meaning:
Official suspension of import and/or export of some specific or all goods, to or from a specific port, country, or region, for political, health, or labor related reasons, for a specified or indefinite period.

Example:
Due to its communist beliefs, the country of Cuba was under a long-term embargo by the United States of America.

Now look it up to understand more, and then make your sentences.

1. _____.
2. _____.
3. _____.

239. WORK-LIFE BALANCE

Meaning:
Work-life balance is a comfortable state of equilibrium achieved between an employee's primary priorities of their employment position and their private lifestyle.

Example:
You must always try to have the perfect work-life balance so that you do not get too bogged down with either.

Now look it up to understand more, and then make your sentences.

1. _____.
2. _____.
3. _____.

240. CAREER

Meaning:

Career is the progress and actions taken by a person throughout a lifetime, especially those related to that person's occupations. A career is often composed of the jobs held, titles earned and work accomplished over a long period of time, rather than just referring to one position.

Example:

After you graduate college and learn everything you need to about your field, you can finally launch a career and have a job that can provide you with a comfortable lifestyle.

Now look it up to understand more, and then make your sentences.

1. _____ .

2. _____ .

3. _____ .

TREASURE BOX 16: UNDERSTAND INSURANCE POLICY

Insurance policy
(1) puts an indemnity cover into effect, (2) serves as a legal evidence of the insurance agreement, (3) sets out the exact terms on which the indemnity cover has been provided, and (4) states associated information such as the (a) specific risks and perils covered, (b) duration of coverage, (c) amount of premium, (d) mode of premium payment, and (e) deductibles, if any.

REVIEW QUIZ

1. The ....of the company was unexpected but we prepared for this moment so we simply worked our plan and adapted.

2. Any time you will be taking on a risky venture it is important to take out an...................... and protect yourself.

3. The amount of insurance ....that is required for insurance coverage depends on a variety of factors.

4. We were rated as the top store in ....satisfaction and had no complaints from customers over the last four months.

5. We were able to improve our market ....by investing heavily in our marketing and advertising as we knew we had a great product.

6. Major corporations take advantage of the opportunity to conduct a ....study on any new investments they make.

7. Venture ....are willing to invest in companies because they can earn a massive return on their investments if these companies are a success.

8. If you want your product to grow you can turn your business into a.................... corporation to find many new customers.

9. If you know of a new company that you think will succeed you may want to take a chance on its ....public offering.

10. The ....became very successful because of her excellent skills in detailing the benefits of the product she was selling to the client, and could often use that skill to close the sale.

11. When I got my new job, I had to report to the human...........department for new worker orientation and to set up my tax information.

12. Don't be too excited because you have been called by a......................, but your chances for the job are higher than those of some other regular candidates that applied directly.

13. Due to its communist beliefs, the country of Cuba was under a long-term ....by the United States of America.

14. The company published its most recent ....plan and distributed it to a group of potential investors and other interested parties.

15. It's very common for individuals who are trying to start their own business to look into finding an ....to provide them with startup money.

16. You must always try to have the perfect ....balance so that you do not get too bogged down with either.

17. After you graduate college and learn everything you need to about your field, you can finally launch a ....and have a job that can provide you with a comfortable lifestyle.

18. You should always know every little detail about any potential .... so that you can be prepared for anything and everything.

19. The return on............... was consistent year after year so we promptly invested more in the company.

20. I would suggest ....as the optimal decision here as the government is inefficient and should not be involved as a rule.

241. WORK ENVIRONMENT

Meaning:
Work environment is the physical geographical location as well as the immediate surroundings of the workplace, such as a construction site or office building.

Example:
You should always try to have the best work environment possible so that you can always be putting in efficient time.

Now look it up to understand more, and then make your sentences.

1. _____.
2. _____.
3. _____.

242. FACE TIME

Meaning:
It is the time you spend at work talking to people directly, not by email, phone, or online.

Example:
My CEO likes to get as much face time as possible with junioremployees.

Now look it up to understand more, and then make your sentences.

1. _____.
2. _____.
3. _____.

243. MANAGERIAL FLEXIBILITY

Definition
The management team's ability to adapt investment decisions, including timing and scale, to existing market conditions as opposed to preset assumptions and goals.

Example:
A mining company might use managerial flexibility in its operations in order to take advantage of rapidly rising mineral prices.

Now look it up to understand more, and then make your sentences.

1. _____.
2. _____.
3. _____.

244. VIRTUAL WORKPLACE

Meaning:
A workplace that has multiple locations, but not necessarily the same all the time, as business is done over email, mail, internet and video. Employees within the company communicate with each other through such technology, as well as the staff communicating with their clients/customers.

Example:
A virtual workplace integrates hardware, people, and online processes.

Now look it up to understand more, and then make your sentences.

1. _____.
2. _____.
3. _____.

245. SABBATICAL

Meaning:
Sabbatical i sa period of time during which someone does not work at his or her regular job and is able to rest, travel, do research, etc.

Example:
She recently returned to work after a two-year sabbatical from her acting career.

Now look it up to understand more, and then make your sentences.

1. _____.
2. _____.
3. _____.

246. THE BALL IS IN SOMEONE'S COURT

Meaning:
If the ball is in someone's court, they have to do something before any progress can be made in a situation.

Example:
We made a reasonable offer for the business acquisition, and now the ball is in their court.

Now look it up to understand more, and then make your sentences.

1. _____.
2. _____.
3. _____.

247. A LONG HAUL

Meaning:
A long haul means something that takes a lot of time and energy.

Example:
It's been a long haul but we've finally got the house looking the way we want it.

Now look it up to understand more, and then make your sentences.

1. _____.
2. _____.
3. _____.

248. SET THE RECORD STRAIGHT

Meaning:
To set the record straight is to tell the true facts that have not been accurately reported.

Example:
Despite the administration's attempts to set the record straight, the scandal refuses to die down.

Now look it up to understand more, and then make your sentences.

1. _____.
2. _____.
3. _____.

249. PUT (SOMETHING) ON THE BACK BURNER

Meaning:
To put (something) on the back burner is to establish something as being a low priority or to give something less or little thought or attention.

Example:
She decided to attend Harvard, where she would study political theory and put her acting career on the back burner.

Now look it up to understand more, and then make your sentences.

1. _____.
2. _____.
3. _____.

250. HAVE YOUR WORK CUT OUT (FOR YOU)

Meaning:
If you have your work cut out, you have something very difficult to complete and possibly in a very short time.

Example:
We're training a completely new team, so we've got our work cut out for us.

Now look it up to understand more, and then make your sentences.

1. _____.
2. _____.
3. _____.

251. UP-AND-COMING

Meaning:
Up-and-coming is used for someone or something likely to develop, become successful, or become popular soon.

Example:
She founded a business school for up-and-coming entrepreneurs.

Now look it up to understand more, and then make your sentences.

1. _____.
2. _____.
3. _____.

252. IN THE DARK (ABOUT SOMEONE OR SOMETHING)

Meaning:
To be **in the dark** means uninformed or ignorant about someone or something.

Example:
I'm in the dark about who is in charge around here.

Now look it up to understand more, and then make your sentences.

1. _____.
2. _____.
3. _____.

253. GLASS CEILING

Meaning:
A Glass ceiling is a nunacknowledged discriminatory and unfair system that prevents some people, especially women, from reaching the most senior positions in a company or organization.

Example:
My friend knew she would never get through the glass ceiling, no matter how long and how hard she worked in her company.

Now look it up to understand more, and then make your sentences.

1. _____.
2. _____.
3. _____.

254. BRAINSTORMING

Meaning:
Brainstorming is the process of generating creative ideas and solutions through intensive and freewheeling group discussion. Every participant is encouraged to think aloud and suggest as many ideas as possible, no matter seemingly how outlandish or bizarre.

Example:
The brainstorming engaged in by our intelligent and creative team resulted in many great ideas for the future of our firm.

Now look it up to understand more, and then make your sentences.

1. _____.
2. _____.
3. _____.

255. Pick someone's brains

Meaning:

To pick someone's brains is to obtain information or ideas by questioning someone closely.

Example:

I'm out of ideas for decorating—let me pick your brain.

Now look it up to understand more, and then make your sentences.

1. _____ .
2. _____ .
3. _____ .

Treasure Box 17: Use appropriate eye contact

Eye contact is one more way that people gauge the trustworthiness of others. If you are not sure how long to hold the other person's gaze, look at their eyes long enough to register what color their eyes are. Eye contact is also critical if you are meeting online, so be sure to look at the other person on the screen, just as if you were meeting in person.

256. RULE OF THUMB

Meaning:
Rule of thumb is a general or approximate principle, procedure, or rule based on experience or practice, as opposed to a specific, scientific calculation or estimate.

Example:
Diversified financial portfoliois certainly an investing rule of thumb.

Now look it up to understand more, and then make your sentences.

1. _____.
2. _____.
3. _____.

257. CALL THE SHOTS

Meaning:
To call the shots is to be in a position of control or authority or to be the person who makes all the important decisions.

Example:
The company was more successful when just one or two people were calling the shots.

Now look it up to understand more, and then make your sentences.

1. _____.
2. _____.
3. _____.

258. ON THE SAME WAVELENGTH

Meaning:

If two people are on the same wavelength, it is easy for them to understand and agree with each other.

Example:

To my surprise, I found that we were absolutely on the same wavelength about most of the important issues.

Now look it up to understand more, and then make your sentences.

1. _____.
2. _____.
3. _____.

259. IN THE RED

Meaning:

To be in the red is referring to a company that is burdened by operating expenses and is unable to generate revenue.

Example:

The newspaper strike put many businesses in the red.

Now look it up to understand more, and then make your sentences.

1. _____.
2. _____.
3. _____.

260. BREATHE DOWN SOMEONE'S NECK

Meaning:
To breathe down someone's neck is to watch closely what someone is doing, in a way that annoys that person.

Example:
If everyone keeps breathing down my neck, it will be very difficult to get my work done.

Now look it up to understand more, and then make your sentences.

1. _____.

2. _____.

3. _____.

REVIEW QUIZ

1. I'm out of ideas for decorating—let me........... your brain.

2. A mining company might use ....flexibility in its operations in order to take advantage of rapidly rising mineral prices.

3. She recently returned to work after a two-year ....from her acting career.

4. A virtual.............. integrates hardware, people, and online processes.

5. She founded a business school for ....-and-coming entrepreneurs.

6. We made a reasonable offer for the business acquisition, and now the........... is in their court.

7. I'm in the............ about who is in charge around here.

8. We're training a completely new team, so we've got our........... cut out for us.

9. My friend knew she would never get through the glass ....no matter how long and how hard she worked in her company.

10. It's been a ....haul but we've finally got the house looking the way we want it.

11. If everyone keeps................. down my neck, it will be very difficult to get my work done.

12. Despite the administration's attempts to ....the record straight, the scandal refuses to die down.

13. She decided to attend Harvard, where she would study political theory and put her acting career on the back................

14. The ....engaged in by our intelligent and creative team resulted in many great ideas for the future of our firm.

15. To my surprise, I found that we were absolutely on the same .... about most of the important issues.

16. Diversified financial portfolios certainly an investing........... of thumb.

17. The newspaper strike put many businesses in the...............

18. You should always try to have the best work ....possible so that you can always be putting in efficient time.

19. My CEO likes to get as much face ....as possible with junior employees.

20. The company was more successful when just one or two people were ....the shots.

261. TWIST SOMEONE'S ARM

Meaning:

To twist someone's arm is to persuade someone to do something that they do not want to do.

Example:

I didn't want to go to the exhibition, but my boss twisted my arm.

Now look it up to understand more, and then make your sentences.

1. _____.
2. _____.
3. _____.

262. SEE EYE TO EYE

Meaning:

To see eye to eye with someone is to agree with someone, or to have the same opinion as them.

Example:

I don't see eye to eye with my business partner on many things.

Now look it up to understand more, and then make your sentences.

1. _____.
2. _____.
3. _____.

263. TALK SHOP

Meaning:
To talk shop is to talk about business or work matters at a social event.

Example:
All right, everyone, we're not here to talk shop. Let's have a good time.

Now look it up to understand more, and then make your sentences.

1. _____.
2. _____.
3. _____.

264. OVERTIME

Meaning:
Work performed by an employee or worker in excess of a basic workday (typically 8 hours a day, 5 days a week) as defined by company rules, job contract, statute, or union (collective) agreement.

Example:
In addition to regular work hours, it is not uncommon for employees of some companies to work overtime in order to get all of the work done required for the day.

Now look it up to understand more, and then make your sentences.

1. _____.
2. _____.
3. _____.

265. CONTRACTUAL RELATIONSHIP

Meaning:
Legal relationship between contracting-parties evidenced by (1) an offer, (2) acceptance of the offer, and a (3) valid (legal and valuable) consideration.

Example:
Existence of a contractual relationship, however, does not necessarily mean the contract is enforceable, that it is not void or not voidable.

Now look it up to understand more, and then make your sentences.

1. _____.
2. _____.
3. _____.

266. VOID CONTRACT

Meaning:
A contract that meets any of the following criteria:
(1) it is illegal from the moment it is made; (2) it is legal but declared null by the courts because it violates a fundamental principle such as fairness, or is contrary to public policy; (3) it becomes void due to changes in law or in government policy; or (4) it has been fully performed.

Example:
The tenants' unpaid balance for their rental home resulted in void contract of their lease; they no longer had a home.

Now look it up to understand more, and then make your sentences.

1. _____.
2. _____.
3. _____.

267. RIFLE APPROACH

Meaning:
This is a marketing strategy that focuses on only one target. That is, a rifle approach attempts to market a product to a small, narrowly defined demographic. On the contrary, a **shotgun approach** attempts to market a product to as many demographics as possible.

Example:
Many have followed the example of South Asia and have now moved on to the rifle approach.

Now look it up to understand more, and then make your sentences.

1. _____.
2. _____.
3. _____.

268. BURN YOUR BRIDGES

Meaning:
To burn your bridges is to permanently and unpleasantly end your relationship with a person or organization.

Example:
If you get mad and quit your job, you'll be burning your bridges behind you. No sense burning your bridges. Be polite and leave quietly.

Now look it up to understand more, and then make your sentences.

1. _____.
2. _____.
3. _____.

269. WHISTLE-BLOWER

Meaning:
A whistle-blower is someone who reports dishonest or illegal activities within an organization to someone in authority.

Example:
The whistle blower had a tough ethical decision to make that he labored over for weeks before finally speaking up.

Now look it up to understand more, and then make your sentences.

1. _____.
2. _____.
3. _____.

270. IN (ALL) GOOD CONSCIENCE

Meaning:
In good conscience means having good motives or displaying motives that will not result in a guilty conscience.

Example:
I could not in good conscience recommend a family member for the job.

Now look it up to understand more, and then make your sentences.

1. _____.
2. _____.
3. _____.

TREASURE BOX 18: ENGAGE IN CHITCHAT

You may think that small talk is a waste of time (and just want the conversation done and over with.) But small talk is important to the art of conversation; a few minutes chatting about the weather helps eliminate your own awkwardness before you ease into more serious topics. Chitchat also makes the other person feel comfortable which will make you more likable.

271. SHOESTRING BUDGET

Meaning:
AShoestring budget is a budget or allotment of resources that is very meager, sparse, or just enough to suit its purpose.

Example:
Unfortunately, due to government cutbacks following the recession, our department has had to produce the same levels of work on a shoestring budget.

Now look it up to understand more, and then make your sentences.

1. _____.

2. _____.

3. _____.

272. ALLOCATION OF RESOURCES

Meaning:

Allocation of resources is a central theme in economics which is essentially a study of how resources are allocated and is associated with economic efficiency and maximization of utility.

Example:

The company diverted a lot of money into the allocation of resources to become as profitable as possible and to be able to protect their initial investment.

Now look it up to understand more, and then make your sentences.

1. _____.
2. _____.
3. _____.

273. ECONOMIC EFFICIENCY

Meaning:

Also called Allocative efficiency is the situation where some people cannot be made better-off by reallocating the resources or goods, without making others worse-off. It indicates that a balance between benefit and loss has been achieved.

Example:

You need to make sure that your business is proficient in economic efficiency so that you can get the most from your product.

Now look it up to understand more, and then make your sentences.

1. _____.
2. _____.
3. _____.

274. MAXIMIZATION OF UTILITY

Meaning:
A theory used in economics that holds the belief that when individuals purchase a good or a service, they strive to obtain the most amount of value possible, while at the same time spending the least amount of money possible. When combined, the consumer is attempting to derive the greatest amount of value from their available funds.

Example:
You should always try and make sure that you are good with utility maximization so that you get the best deal

Now look it up to understand more, and then make your sentences.

1. _____.
2. _____.
3. _____.

275. BARGAINING POWER

Meaning:
Bargaining power in negotiating isthe capacity of one party to dominate the other due to its influence, power, size, or status, or through a combination of different persuasion tactics.

Example:
Because of her premium standing with the company, she knew she had the Bargaining Power necessary to secure the deal.

Now look it up to understand more, and then make your sentences.

1. _____.
2. _____.
3. _____.

276. BRAND AWARENESS

Meaning:
Brand awareness is the extent to which a brand is recognized by potential customers, and is correctly associated with a particular product.

Example:
Brand awareness is the primary goal of advertising in the early months or years of a product's introduction.

Now look it up to understand more, and then make your sentences.

1. _____.
2. _____.
3. _____.

277. BRAND MANAGEMENT

Meaning:
Brand management is the process of maintaining, improving, and upholding a brand so that the name is associated with positive results.

Example:
Our new brand management strategy was working great and our brands remained very prestigious and a cut above the rest.

Now look it up to understand more, and then make your sentences.

1. _____.
2. _____.
3. _____.

278. Brand piracy

Meaning:
Brand piracy is a situation where certain products that have names or logos that are similar to those of recognized businesses.
They can be mistaken for the original brand names, mislead customers and they break trademark laws.

Example:
Brand piracy results in expensive lawsuits.

Now look it up to understand more, and then make your sentences.

1. _____.

2. _____.

3. _____.

279. Trademark Law

Meaning:
Trademark Law governs disputes between business owners over the names, logos, and other means they use to identify their products and services in the marketplace.

Example:
Trademark law gives trademark ownersa duty to police their marks and to prevent other parties from infringing on their trademarks.

Now look it up to understand more, and then make your sentences.

1. _____.

2. _____.

3. _____.

280. TRADEMARK INFRINGEMENT

Meaning:
Trademark infringement is the violation of the terms of trademark of another entity by encroaching on the rights and privileges provided to the entity that owns the property.

Example:
A lawsuit may be filed for trademark infringement as long as the party filing the complaint has registered (even if not registered in some cases) the trademark properly.

Now look it up to understand more, and then make your sentences.

1. _____.
2. _____.
3. _____.

Review Quiz

1. All right, everyone, we're not here to............... shop. Let's have a good time.

2. I could not in good ....recommend a family member for the job.

3. If you get mad and quit your job, you'll be................ your bridges behind you. Be polite and leave quietly.

4. The whistle ....had a tough ethical decision to make that he labored over for weeks before finally speaking up.

5. Unfortunately, due to government cutbacks following the recession, our department has had to produce the same levels of work on a.................. budget.

6. The company diverted a lot of money into the.................. of resources to become as profitable as possible and to be able to protect their initial investment.

7. In addition to regular work hours, it is not uncommon for employees of some companies to work ....in order to get all of the work done required for the day.

8. The tenants' unpaid balance for their rental home resulted in void ....of their lease; they no longer had a home.

9. You need to make sure that your business is proficient in economic.................. so that you can get the most from your product.

10. Many have followed the example of South Asia and have now moved on to the rifle......................

11. Because of her premium standing with the company, she knew she had the ....Power necessary to secure the deal.

12. Brand ....results in expensive lawsuits.

13. Brand ....is the primary goal of advertising in the early months or years of a product's introduction.

14. Our new brand ....strategy was working great and our brands remained very prestigious and a cut above the rest.

15. Trademark law gives trademark owners a duty to police their marks and to..................... other parties from infringing on their trademarks.

16. A lawsuit may be filed for........... infringement as long as the party filing the complaint has registered (even if not registered in some cases) the trademark properly.

17. Existence of a ....relationship, however, does not necessarily mean the contract is enforceable, that it is not void or not voidable.

18. I don't................ eye to eye with my business partner on many things.

19. I didn't want to go to the exhibition, but my boss................ my arm.

20. You should always try and make sure that you are good with utility................ so that you get the best deal

281. COMPLIANCE

Meaning:
Certification or confirmation that the doer of an action such as the writer of an audit report, or the manufacturer or supplier of a product, meets the requirements of accepted practices, legislation, prescribed rules and regulations, specified standards, or the terms of a contract.

Example:
When you are employed with a company, they require you to be in compliance with all policies and procedures at all times.

Now look it up to understand more, and then make your sentences.

1. _____.
2. _____.
3. _____.

282. CONCEALED UNEMPLOYMENT

Meaning:
Concealed unemployment is a situation where people who are out of work are not counted in official unemployment statistics.

Example:
The non-inclusion of concealed unemployment in overall unemployment numbers allows for a higher perceived rate of employment.

Now look it up to understand more, and then make your sentences.

1. _____.
2. _____.
3. _____.

283. CONCURRENT EMPLOYMENT

Meaning:
In general, concurrent employment is defined as an employment situation in which an employee has several personnel assignments with one organization.

Example:
Some key functional areas together with the technological framework provide the necessary infrastructure to support concurrent employment.

Now look it up to understand more, and then make your sentences.

1. _____.
2. _____.
3. _____.

284. BAGGAGE ALLOWANCE

Meaning:
Baggage allowance is the amount of checked or carry-on luggage the airline will allow per passenger.

Example:
The general baggage allowance per passenger depends on the policies of the particular airline.

Now look it up to understand more, and then make your sentences.

1. _____.
2. _____.
3. _____.

285. BAGGAGE CLAIM

Meaning:
This is the designated area at an airport or seaport where passengers can identify and pick up their checked-in baggage.

Example:
A typical baggage claim area contains conveyor systems that deliver checked baggage to the passenger.

Now look it up to understand more, and then make your sentences.

1. _____.
2. _____.
3. _____.

TREASURE BOX 19: BE PUNCTUAL

Being late for an appointment starts you off at a disadvantage. If you are meeting in person, plan to arrive a little early so you can find a parking space and collect your thoughts. If you are participating in a web meeting, eliminate distractions ahead of time and be ready to log in as soon as the meeting starts.

286. SUSTAINABILITY

Meaning:

Sustainability a continuous development or growth of economy, without significant deterioration of the environment and depletion of natural resources on which human well-being depends.

Example:

The company proposed a new manufacturing process based on its improved sustainability over the previous process which required use of a rare mineral.

Now look it up to understand more, and then make your sentences.

1. _____.
2. _____.
3. _____.

287. SUSTAINABLE COMPETITIVE ADVANTAGE

Meaning:

This is a long-term competitive advantage that is not easily duplicable or surpassable by the competitors.

Example:

A firm manipulates the various resources over which it has direct control and these resources have the ability to generate sustainable competitive advantage.

Now look it up to understand more, and then make your sentences.

1. _____.
2. _____.
3. _____.

288. BUYING MOTIVES

Meaning:
The combination of facts and the emotional state of a person that generates a feeling within them that they need to purchase an item, as well as the factors that influence their eventual choice of a particular product.

Example:
The marketing team of a business will often strategically take into account key buying motives within a target consumer group in order to enhance sales of their product.

Now look it up to understand more, and then make your sentences.

1. _____.
2. _____.
3. _____.

289. RISK MANAGEMENT

Meaning:
Risk management isthe identification, analysis, assessment, control, and avoidance, minimization, or elimination of unacceptable risks. An organization may use risk assumption, risk avoidance, risk retention, risk transfer, or any other strategy (or combination of strategies) in proper management of future events.

Example:
The company couldn't afford any more losses, so they sought out the best and brightest risk management experts to help them get back on track.

Now look it up to understand more, and then make your sentences.

1. _____.
2. _____.
3. _____.

290. RISK ASSUMPTION

Meaning:
Practice of absorbing minor losses but protecting against catastrophic losses such as due to robbery or fire by buying insurance cover.

Example:
The judge ruled that the assumption of risk was inherent in the job description when the worker sued the company.

Now look it up to understand more, and then make your sentences.

1. _____.
2. _____.
3. _____.

291. RISK AVOIDANCE

Meaning:
Risk avoidance is a risk management technique that involves taking steps to remove a hazard, engage in alternative activity, or end a specific exposure.

Example:
The owner of the new company decided against the purchase at this time because of the possible loss it would suffer if the new product did not sell, which he considered a risk avoidance and felt good about his decision.

Now look it up to understand more, and then make your sentences.

1. _____.
2. _____.
3. _____.

92. RISK TRANSFER

Meaning:
Risk management strategy in which an insurable risk is shifted to another party by means of an insurance policy.

Example:
By partnering with another company we were able to do a risk transfer as they would be underwriting the construction on the new building.

Now look it up to understand more, and then make your sentences.

1. _____.
2. _____.
3. _____.

293. RISK RETENTION

Meaning:
A form of self-insurance employed by organizations which have determined that the cost of transferring a risk to an insurance company is greater over time than the cost of retaining the risk and paying for losses out of their own reserve fund.

Example:
Though he was injured at his self-owned construction company in he was confident that his risk retention would cover any costs associated with being seriously injured on the job.

Now look it up to understand more, and then make your sentences.

1. _____.
2. _____.
3. _____.

294. UNDERWRITING

Meaning:
Underwriting is the acceptance by a financial institution of the financial risks involved in a particular transaction. In other words, underwriting is insuring.

Example:
You should always be wary of any underwriting unless you have full faith in that company over a good period of time.

Now look it up to understand more, and then make your sentences.

1. _____.
2. _____.
3. _____.

295. RISK MITIGATION/RISK REDUCTION

Meaning:
The process by which an organization introduces specific measures to minimize or eliminate unacceptable risks associated with its operations.

Example:
Business executives that practice risk mitigation protect themselves and their companies from unnecessary lawsuits and/or keeping their business from going bankrupt.

Now look it up to understand more, and then make your sentences.

1. _____.
2. _____.
3. _____.

296. RISK PROPENSITY

Meaning:
Risk propensity is the degree to which a decision maker is willing to take chances with respect to risk of loss.

Example:
Findings have suggested that risk taking propensity may not be a distinguishing characteristic of entrepreneurs.

Now look it up to understand more, and then make your sentences.

1. _____.
2. _____.
3. _____.

297. RISK OF LOSS

Meaning:
Probability that one will have to bear the costs associated with a damage, destruction, injury, or an inability to locate documents, goods, or other property.

Example:
The mayor said thatthe proposed relocation could expose the city to undue risk of loss of irreplaceable documents.

Now look it up to understand more, and then make your sentences.

1. _____.
2. _____.
3. _____.

298. CRISIS MANAGEMENT

Meaning:
Set of procedures applied in handling, containment, and resolution of an emergency in planned and coordinated steps.

Example:
You should always try and keep a cool head when you are dealing with crisis management and not make any brash decisions.

Now look it up to understand more, and then make your sentences.

1. _____.
2. _____.
3. _____.

299. RISK FREE INVESTMENT

Meaning:
Security, such as a government bond or certificate of deposit (CD), that is generally considered to be free from risk of monetary loss and is used as a benchmark for evaluating investment proposals.

Example:
His small firm specializes in single family houses and risk free investments

Now look it up to understand more, and then make your sentences.

1. _____.
2. _____.
3. _____.

300. FIDUCIARY

Meaning:
A fiduciary is responsible for managing the assets of another person, or of a group of people. Asset managers, bankers, accountants, executors, board members, and corporate officers can all be considered fiduciaries when entrusted in good faith with the responsibility of managing another party's assets.

Example:
When choosing a fiduciary to handle your personal funds and loans, you want someone who is very trustworthy and has your goals in mind.

Now look it up to understand more, and then make your sentences.

1. _____.

2. _____.

3. _____.

TREASURE BOX 20: GET MORE SLEEP TO APPEAR MORE INTELLIGENT

New research recently uncovered one trick that's simple to implement. To look smarter, simply sleep more according to a recent study out of the University of St. Andrews in Scotland.

The study, found that being well-rested isn't just good for your mood, your health, and your cognitive function, it also causes others to see you as more intelligent. When you especially need to impress the next day, perhaps for a job interview or big presentation and you really want to look your most competent and compelling, these are the times you really ought to try to get enough sleep.

REVIEW QUIZ

1. When choosing a ....to handle your personal funds and loans, you want someone who is very trustworthy and has your goals in mind.

2. A typical baggage............... area contains conveyor systems that deliver checked baggage to the passenger.

3. The general baggage ....per passenger depends on the policies of the particular airline.

4. Business executives that practice ....mitigation protect themselves and their companies from unnecessary lawsuits and/or keeping their business from going bankrupt.

5. The non-inclusion of ....unemployment in overall unemployment numbers allows for a higher perceived rate of employment.

6. The company proposed a new manufacturing process based on its improved ....over the previous process which required use of a rare mineral.

7. The company couldn't afford any more losses so they sought out the best and brightest ....management experts to help them get back on track.

8. When you are employed with a company, they require you to be in ....with all policies and procedures at all times.

9. You should always try and keep a cool head when you are dealing with ....management and not make any brash decisions.

10. Some key functional areas together with the technological framework provide the necessary infrastructure to support .... employment.

11. The owner of the new company decided against the purchase at this time which he considered a................ avoidance and felt good about his decision.

12. The marketing team of a business will often strategically take into account key buying............... within a target consumer group in order to enhance sales of their product.

13. By partnering with another company we were able to do a .... transfer as they would be underwriting the construction on the new building.

14. The mayor said that the proposed relocation could expose the city to undue................. of loss of irreplaceable documents.

15. Though he was injured at his self-owned construction company in he was confident that his............. retention would cover any costs associated with being seriously injured on the job.

16. The judge ruled that the assumption of............... was inherent in the job description.

17. You should always be wary of any ....unless you have full faith in that company over a good period of time.

18. Findings have suggested that ....taking propensity may not be a distinguishing characteristic of entrepreneurs.

19. A firm manipulates the various resources over which it has direct control and these resources have the ability to generate sustainable .... advantage.

20. His small firm specializes in single family houses and ....free investments

301. ACCULTURATION

Meaning:
Socialization processes through which new employees learn, adjust to, and internalize the corporate culture.

Example:
Progressive organizations allow for sufficient acculturation time and help newcomers through orientation sessions and by facilitating learning.

Now look it up to understand more, and then make your sentences.

1. _____.
2. _____.
3. _____.

302. PREAMBLE

Meaning:
Introductory part (recital) of a bill, constitution, or statute that sets out in details the underlying facts and assumptions, and explains its intent and objectives. Its objective is to clarify the meaning or purpose of the operative part of the text in case of an ambiguity or dispute.

Example:
Preamble prevails only where it provides a clear and definite interpretation whereas the meaning of the enacting words is indefinite or unclear.

Now look it up to understand more, and then make your sentences.

1. _____.
2. _____.
3. _____.

303. DISCRETE

Meaning:
Discrete means individually recognizable and countable, distinct and separate from the similar items, finite and non-continuous.

Example:
The company liked to keep its different manufacturing lines as discrete units to avoid any confusion over the use of different processes.

Now look it up to understand more, and then make your sentences.

1. _____.
2. _____.
3. _____.

304. JOB ANALYSIS

Meaning:
Detailed examination of the (1) tasks (performance elements) that make up a job (employee role), (2) conditions under which they are performed, and (3) what the job requires in terms of aptitudes (potential for achievement), attitudes (behavior characteristics), knowledge, skills, and the physical condition of the employee.

Example:
Comprehensive job analysis begins with the study of the organization itself: its purpose, design and structure, inputs and outputs, internal and external environments, and resource constraints.

Now look it up to understand more, and then make your sentences.

1. _____.
2. _____.
3. _____.

305. LABOR FORCE

Meaning:

Labor force is the number of workers in a firm or number of individuals in an economy who either are employed or are seeking employment.

Example:

The senior executives searched exhaustively for ways to save the company money without resorting to layoffs because they wanted to avoid the negative impact it may have on the labor force.

Now look it up to understand more, and then make your sentences.

1. _____.
2. _____.
3. _____.

306. BACK IS TO THE WALL

Meaning:

When your back is to/against the wall, you are in a bad position in which you are forced to do something in order to avoid failure.

Example:

We knew that with so little time and money left to finish the project we had our backs to the wall.

Now look it up to understand more, and then make your sentences.

1. _____.
2. _____.
3. _____.

307. Shortcoming

Meaning:
Shortcoming is a weakness in someone's character or a personal bad feature or a defect in something.

Examples:

1. Her lack of attention to detail is her biggest shortcoming.
2. The main/major shortcoming of this camera is that it uses up batteries quickly.

Now look it up to understand more, and then make your sentences.

1. _____.
2. _____.
3. _____.

308. A Window Into/On

Meaning:
A window into/on something or situation is something that makes it possible to see or understand something clearly.

Examples:
1. This knowledge opens a window into your opponent's mind.
2. The book gives the reader a window on war.

Now look it up to understand more, and then make your sentences.

1. _____.
2. _____.
3. _____.

309. FALL THROUGH

Meaning:
Business or plans may fall through if it fails to occur or to be unsuccessful.

Example:
I hope our plans won't fall through.

Now look it up to understand more, and then make your sentences.

1. _____.
2. _____.
3. _____.

310. AFFLUENZA

Meaning:
A social theory claiming that individuals with very privileged and wealthy backgrounds sometimes struggle to determine the difference between right and wrong due to the nature of their upbringing. It is also known as **sudden-wealth syndrome**.

Example:
Attorneys argued that the teen suffered from affluenza since he did not know right from wrong due to his wealthy upbringing.

Now look it up to understand more, and then make your sentences.

1. _____.
2. _____.
3. _____.

311. FOOT IN THE DOOR

Meaning:
It is a method of getting an individual to agree to something by first asking them for a smaller request.

Example:
The foot in the door tactic is often used by salespeople.

Now look it up to understand more, and then make your sentences.

1. _____.
2. _____.
3. _____.

312. INGENIOUS

Meaning:
It means something that is marked by originality, resourcefulness, and cleverness in conception or execution.

Example:
It was ingenious of him to arrange the schedule so precisely.

Now look it up to understand more, and then make your sentences.

1. _____.
2. _____.
3. _____.

313. MOVERS AND SHAKERS

Meaning:
Movers and shakers are people who are active or powerful in some field.

Examples:
1. The movers and shakers of the computer industry.
2. Political movers and shakers.

Now look it up to understand more, and then make your sentences.

1. _____.
2. _____.
3. _____.

314. SUPPRESS

Meaning:
To Suppress is to slow or stop the growth, development, or normal functioning of something or activity.

Example:
ABC is a drug that suppresses the immune system.

Now look it up to understand more, and then make your sentences.

1. _____.
2. _____.
3. _____.

315. GUIDELINE

Meaning:
It is a rule or instruction that shows or tells how something should be done.

Example:
The government has issued new guidelines for following a healthy and balanced diet.

Now look it up to understand more, and then make your sentences.

1. _____.
2. _____.
3. _____.

TREASURE BOX 21: INTERNALIZE YOUR ENGLISH

The path between the learning event and the direct results passes through something called INTERNALIZING. How do you internalize? Pass what you learn through your own filter. Ask yourself "Is this good for me? Is this applicable to my situation?" It can happen that out of this state of curiosity you'll discover what you want. For a book, it might be a sentence. For a movie, it might be the opener or the ending. Whichever it is, it is your value out of it i.e. being able to utilize what you have learned.

316. SCOPE

Meaning:
Scope means, the area that is included in or dealt with by something.

Example:
I was impressed by the size and scope of the book.

Now look it up to understand more, and then make your sentences.

1. _____.
2. _____.
3. _____.

317. SCOPE OF WORK

Meaning:
This is the division of work to be performed under a contract or subcontract in the completion of a project, typically broken out into specific tasks with deadlines.

Example:
The scope of work was incredible and I did not think we would be able to finish it before the end of the day.

Now look it up to understand more, and then make your sentences.

1. _____.
2. _____.
3. _____.

318. FISCAL

Meaning:
It means something relating to public revenues (taxation), public spending, debt, and finance.

Example:
Relating to the government and their spending habits, one could come to the conclusion of a 'fiscal cliff', resulting in negative impacts for society, causing debt and loss of work.

Now look it up to understand more, and then make your sentences.

1. _____.
2. _____.
3. _____.

319. MONETARY

Meaning:
Monetary relates to money and how it is supplied to, and circulates in, an economy.

Example:
When I took the job I was not horribly impressed with the monetary gain that I was able to reach in the beginning.

Now look it up to understand more, and then make your sentences.

1. _____.
2. _____.
3. _____.

320. EFFECTIVE

Meaning:
1. Having the desired result.

Example:
The medicine was effective in curing his infection.
2. In effect or starting at a particular time.

Example:
The new law about traffic violations is effective starting today, so from now on, be extra careful about obeying the speed limit.

Now look it up to understand more, and then make your sentences.

1. _____.
2. _____.
3. _____.

REVIEW QUIZ

1. ABC is a drug that.................... the immune system.

2. Comprehensive................ analysis begins with the study of the organization itself: its purpose, design and structure, inputs and outputs, internal and external environments, and resource constraints.

3. The senior executives searched exhaustively for ways to save the company money without resorting to layoffs because they wanted to avoid the negative impact it may have on the .... force.

4. Progressive organizations allow for sufficient acculturation time and help ....through orientation sessions and by facilitating learning.

5. Preamble prevails only where it provides a clear and definite .... whereas the meaning of the enacting words is indefinite or unclear.

6. The.................. and shakers of the computer industry.

7. The government has issued new..................... for following a healthy and balanced diet.

8. I was impressed by the size and............. of the book.

9. When I took the job I was not horribly impressed with the monetary ....that I was able to reach in the beginning.

10. The............ of work was incredible and I did not think we would be able to finish it before the end of the day.

11. The company liked to keep its different manufacturing lines as............ units to avoid any confusion over the use of different processes.

12. We knew that with so little time and money left to finish the project we had our.................. to the wall.

13. The main/major ....of this camera is that it uses up batteries quickly.

14. This knowledge opens a ....into your opponent's mind.

15. I hope our plans won't.................. through.

16. The new law about traffic violations is ....starting today, so from now on, be extra careful about obeying the speed limit.

17. Attorneys argued that the teen suffered from ....since he did not know right from wrong due to his wealthy upbringing.

18. The.............. in the door tactic is often used by salespeople.

19. It was ....of him to arrange the schedule so precisely.

20. Relating to the government and their spending habits, one could come to the conclusion of a.................. cliff, resulting in negative impacts for society, causing debt and loss of work.

321. SETBACKS

Meaning:
It is a problem that makes progress more difficult or success less likely.

Example:
Despite some early setbacks, they eventually became a successful company.

Now look it up to understand more, and then make your sentences.

1. _____.
2. _____.
3. _____.

322. STINT

Meaning:
Stint is a period of time spent doing a certain job or activity.

Example:
He had a brief stint as a mail carrier.

Now look it up to understand more, and then make your sentences.

1. _____.
2. _____.
3. _____.

323. UNDERLIE

Meaning:
Underlie means to form the basis or foundation of an idea or a process.

Example:
Careful planning underlies all our decisions.

Now look it up to understand more, and then make your sentences.

1. _____.
2. _____.
3. _____.

324. LIVING ON BORROWED TIME

Meaning:
This phrase means to continue to be alive after you were expected to die.

Example:
After his heart attack, my grandfather always felt that he was living on borrowed time.

Now look it up to understand more, and then make your sentences.

1. _____.
2. _____.
3. _____.

325. THE TIME IS RIPE

Meaning:
If the time is ripe for something, it is a good time to do it or for it to happen.

Example:
Many employers feel the time is ripe to give workforces a bigger share of the profits they have helped to create.

Now look it up to understand more, and then make your sentences.

1. _____.
2. _____.
3. _____.

326. WORKING AGAINST THE CLOCK

Meaning:
This expression is used in order to do or finish something before a particular time.

Example:
On our last project, we were working/racing against the clock.

Now look it up to understand more, and then make your sentences.

1. _____.
2. _____.
3. _____.

327. IN THE INTERIM (BETWEEN THINGS)

Meaning:

This phrase means in the meantime or in the time between the ending of something and the beginning of something else.

Example:

In the interim between her morning and afternoon classes, Susan rushed home to get a book she had forgotten.

Now look it up to understand more, and then make your sentences.

1. _____.
2. _____.
3. _____.

328: REVOLVING LINE OF CREDIT/REVOLVING CREDIT

Meaning:

An agreement by a bank to lend a specific amount to a borrower and to allow that amount to be borrowed again once it has been repaid.

Example:

A revolving line of credit can seriously dig your credit worthiness in the eyes of credit bureaus if you have too many of them.

Now look it up to understand more, and then make your sentences.

1. _____.
2. _____.
3. _____.

329. KEEP YOUR EYE ON THE BALL

Meaning:
It means that you don't ever lose sight of what you want to achieve Keeping your eye on the ball is all about keeping your wits about you, paying attention to what's happening.

Example:
If you want to get along in this office, you're going to have to keep your eye on the ball.

Now look it up to understand more, and then make your sentences.

1. _____.
2. _____.
3. _____.

330. GET (HOLD OF) THE WRONG END OF THE STICK

Meaning:
To get the wrong end of the stick is to not understand a situation correctly.

Example:
Her friend saw us arrive at the party together and got hold of the wrong end of the stick.

Now look it up to understand more, and then make your sentences.

1. _____.
2. _____.
3. _____.

TREASURE BOX 22: BIG WORDS

If you're a fan of using big words to demonstrate the breadth of your vocabulary and the brilliance of your thinking, be warned: Studies show that using fancy words when simple ones will do is a sure-fire way to end up looking dumb. So, remember that simplicity and clarity are generally a better signal of mastery than flowery language.

331. OVERHEAD /OVERHEAD COSTS

Meaning:
In finance this means costs that result from having and maintaining a business.

Example:
Her company has very little overhead.

Now look it up to understand more, and then make your sentences.

1. _____.
2. _____.
3. _____.

332. EMBEZZLE

Meaning:
To embezzle means to fraudulently appropriate an asset for one's own use.

Example:
He was caught embezzling money from his clients.

Now look it up to understand more, and then make your sentences.

1. _____.
2. _____.
3. _____.

333. KICKBACK

Meaning:
This is a portion of an income demanded as a bribe by an official for facilitating the job or order from which the income is realized.

Example:
The corporate world is tough. It may be tempting to beat out the competition by greasing a few palms or giving kickbacks.

Now look it up to understand more, and then make your sentences.

1. _____.
2. _____.
3. _____.

334. ABOVEBOARD

Meaning:

Aboveboard means open, honest, and legal.

Example:

The committee tried to be fair and aboveboard in its hiring.

Now look it up to understand more, and then make your sentences.

1. _____.
2. _____.
3. _____.

335. GOLDEN HANDCUFFS

Meaning:

Inducements offered to a key employee or a former owner to continue working with a firm. These incentives may take the form of a higher salary, added-on benefits, stock option, and/or lump sum bonus.

Example:

Golden handcuffs are common in industries where highly-compensated employees are likely to move from company to company.

Now look it up to understand more, and then make your sentences.

1. _____.
2. _____.
3. _____.

336. GOLDEN HANDSHAKES

Meaning:
Golden handshakes are financial payments given to employees that are forced to leave, usually due to a restructuring of the organization.

Example:
The executive is normally eligible for a golden handshake regardless of the circumstances under which he/she left the company.

Now look it up to understand more, and then make your sentences.

1. _____.
2. _____.
3. _____.

337. TEAM PLAYER

Meaning:
It means someone who cares more about helping a group or team to succeed than about his or her individual success.

Example:
Ted is a team player. I am sure that he will cooperate with us.

Now look it up to understand more, and then make your sentences.

1. _____.
2. _____.
3. _____.

338. PASS THE BUCK

Meaning:

Passing the buck means to shift blame or responsibility onto another.

Example:

Whenever he is blamed for anything, he tries to pass the buck.

Now look it up to understand more, and then make your sentences.

1. _____.
2. _____.
3. _____.

339. GO PEAR-SHAPED

Meaning:

If a plan goes pear-shaped, it fails.

Example:

We had arranged to be in France that weekend but it all went pear-shaped.

Now look it up to understand more, and then make your sentences.

1. _____.
2. _____.
3. _____.

340. USE ONE'S (OWN) INITIATIVE

Meaning:
If you use your (own) initiative, you decide for yourself what to do instead of waiting to be told by someone else.

Example:
If problems occur, you should use your own initiative to come up with a solution.

Now look it up to understand more, and then make your sentences.

1. _____.
2. _____.
3. _____.

REVIEW QUIZ

1. Many employers feel the time is................. to give workforces a bigger share of the profits they have helped to create.

2. In the ....between her morning and afternoon classes, Susan rushed home to get a book she had forgotten.

3. On our last project, we were working/racing............ the clock.

4. A revolving line of credit can seriously dig your credit ....in the eyes of credit bureaus if you have too many of them.

5. We had arranged to be in France that weekend but it all went.................. shaped.

6. If you want to get along in this office, you're going to have to keep your.............. on the ball.

7. If problems occur, you should use your own ....to come up with a solution.

8. Her friend saw us arrive at the party together and got hold of the................... end of the stick.

9. Her company has very little............................

10. He was ....embezzling money from his clients.

11. The corporate world is tough. It may be tempting to beat out the competition by ....a few palms or giving kickbacks.

12. The committee tried to be fair and ....in its hiring.

13. Golden ....are common in industries where highly-compensated employees are likely to move from company to company.

14. The executive is normally eligible for a golden ....regardless of the circumstances under which he/she left the company.

15. Despite some early.................., they eventually became a successful company.

16. He had a brief ....as a mail carrier.

17. Ted is a.................... player. I am sure that he will cooperate with us.

18. Careful planning................ all our decisions.

19. After his heart attack, my grandfather always felt that he was living on ....time.

20. Whenever he is blamed for anything, he tries to ....the buck.

341. INCENTIVES

Meaning:
An incentive means something that encourages a person to do something or to work harder.

Example:
Our salespeople are given financial incentives for reaching their quotas.

Now look it up to understand more, and then make your sentences.

1. _____.
2. _____.
3. _____.

QUICK REVIEW QUIZ!

What are the differences between, incentives, benefits and remunerations?

342. PROPRIETARY

Meaning:
It means used, made, or sold only by the particular person or company that has the legal right to do so.

Example:
Every computer comes with the manufacturer's proprietary software.

Now look it up to understand more, and then make your sentences.

1. _____.
2. _____.
3. _____.

343. FRUGAL

Meaning:
It means to be careful about spending money or using things when you do not need to.

Example:
She is rich, but she is very frugal with her money.

Now look it up to understand more, and then make your sentences.

1. _____.
2. _____.
3. _____.

344. PROSPER

Meaning:
To prosper is to become very successful usually by making a lot of money.

Example:
She prospered as a real estate agent.

Now look it up to understand more, and then make your sentences.

1. _____.
2. _____.
3. _____.

345. DEPENDABILITY

Meaning:

In quality control, it means the degree to which an item is capable of performing its required function at any randomly chosen time during its specified operating period, disregarding non-operation related influences.

Example:

You should be someone that others say has high dependability so that they can rely on you in times of need.

Now look it up to understand more, and then make your sentences.

1. _____.
2. _____.
3. _____.

TREASURE BOX 23: DECIDE WHAT A CAREER IS FOR

There's much talk about a work/life balance. Making a living is part of making a life. Your career should be aligned with who you are at a fundamental level no less than any other aspect of your life is. Your personal goal should be to maximize happiness, pleasure and meaning, in both yourself and others. Figure out what you want out of life and then figure out what role your career can play in making it happen.

346. OPTIMISTIC

Meaning:
To be optimistic means having or showing hope for the future or expecting good things to happen or to be hopeful even when the situation looks impossible.

Example:
He has an optimistic view of the company's future.

Now look it up to understand more, and then make your sentences.

1. _____.
2. _____.
3. _____.

347. EXPERTISE

Meaning:
This is a special skill or knowledge that an expert has.

Example:
The company has no environmental expertise.

Now look it up to understand more, and then make your sentences.

1. _____.
2. _____.
3. _____.

348. BENCHMARK

Meaning:

It a standard or a set of standards, used as a point of reference for evaluating performance or level of quality.

Example:

A man's ability to keep his word even though there is no legal document is a benchmark of his good character.

Now look it up to understand more, and then make your sentences.

1. _____.
2. _____.
3. _____.

349. INTERVENE

Meaning:

To intervene is to become involved in something such as a conflict in order to have an influence on what happens.

Example:

The military had to intervene to restore order.

Now look it up to understand more, and then make your sentences.

1. _____.
2. _____.
3. _____.

350. OFFSHOOT

Meaning:
Offshoot is something such as a business that develops from something larger.

Example:
The business started as an offshoot of an established fashion design company.

Now look it up to understand more, and then make your sentences.

1. _____.
2. _____.
3. _____.

351. LATERAL THINKING

Meaning:
It means idea generation and problem solving technique in which new concepts are created by looking at things in novel ways. Lateral thinking provokes fresh ideas or changes the frame of reference.

Example:
The lateral thinking exhibited by the new research team showed their creativity, originality, and innovation as they solved the problem.

Now look it up to understand more, and then make your sentences.

1. _____.
2. _____.
3. _____.

352. INCOME STATEMENT

Meaning:
It itemizes the revenues and expenses of past that led to the current profit or loss, and indicate what may be done to improve the results.

Example:
My manager was worried because he would be getting his income statement today and sees how he was doing for the company.

Now look it up to understand more, and then make your sentences.

1. _____.
2. _____.
3. _____.

353. RECRUITMENT

Meaning:
Recruitment is the process of finding and hiring the best-qualified candidate from within or outside of an organization for a job opening, in a timely and cost effective manner.

Examples:
The initial recruitment brought many seemingly qualified candidates into the hiring pool but unfortunately the hiring manager still needed to choose only one.

Now look it up to understand more, and then make your sentences.

1. _____.
2. _____.
3. _____.

354. VICIOUS CIRCLE

Meaning:
It is a repeating situation or condition in which one problem causes another problem that makes the first problem worse.

Example:
We're trapped in a vicious circle.

Now look it up to understand more, and then make your sentences.

1. _____.
2. _____.
3. _____.

355. OPEN DOOR POLICY

Meaning:
This is the Management practice whereby all employees have direct access to the senior executives without going through several gatekeepers or layers of bureaucracy.

Example:
The senior members of the firm had an open door policy, so anyone who wanted to bring something up with them just had to walk through the door and ask.

Now look it up to understand more, and then make your sentences.

1. _____.
2. _____.
3. _____.

356. RIPPLE EFFECT

Meaning:
This is a situation in which one event causes a series of other events to happen.

Example:
These costs will have a huge/major ripple effect on the economy.

Now look it up to understand more, and then make your sentences.

1. _____.
2. _____.
3. _____.

357: OMBUDSMAN

Meaning:
Government official appointed to investigate citizen's complaints against government officials, large public and private corporations, and/or print and broadcast media.

Example:
After the local resident filed a scathing complaint against the city, an ombudsman hurriedly arrived to review the case, and begin their investigation.

Now look it up to understand more, and then make your sentences.

1. _____.
2. _____.
3. _____.

358. HEDGE FUND

Meaning:
Hedge fund is an exceptionally risky and largely unregulated investment partnership which employs aggressive leverage to multiply gains or losses from fluctuations in the prices of financial instruments such as bonds, notes and securities.

Example:
The hedge fund market thrived with the new players that were able to make strategic guesses backed by legitimate analysis.

Now look it up to understand more, and then make your sentences.

1. _____.
2. _____.
3. _____.

359. INFLATION

Meaning:
Inflation may be defined as a rapid **increase in prices**, as over months or years, and mirrored in the correspondingly decreasing purchasing power of the **currency**.

Example:
While some people believe storing their cash in a safe will keep it secure, the value of their money will likely decline over time due to inflation

Now look it up to understand more, and then make your sentences.

1. _____.
2. _____.
3. _____.

360. DEFLATION

Meaning:

Deflation is the opposite of inflation and it may be described as the downturn in an economic cycle caused by circumstances, or brought about by government policies. Deflation is characterized by (1) increase in citizens' purchasing power due to the falling prices, (2) decrease in wages, or slowdown in their increase, due to falling levels of employment, (3) decrease in availability of credit due to higher interest rates and/or restricted money supply, and (4) decrease in imports due to lack of demand.

Example:

The economic deflation was beneficial as far as being able to purchase goods cheaper, but wages also decreased and fewer jobs were available.

Now look it up to understand more, and then make your sentences.

1. _____.
2. _____.
3. _____.

TREASURE BOX. 24: KEEP LEARNING

Obviously you need to learn in order to succeed in your career. But how you learn and what you learn are both essential factors. As for how you learn, having the right frame of mind can help you learn much faster. Have a natural curiosity about the world, let everything be your teacher, and don't limit yourself to learning only those things that are of immediate value to you. As for what to learn, these depends on your chosen career, so talk with some successful people in your desired field and ask what skills helped them succeed and how they developed those skills.

REVIEW QUIZ

1. He has an ....view of the company's future.

2. The company has no ....expertise.

3. The business started as an ....of an established fashion designs company.

4. A man's ability to keep his word even though there is no legal document is a ....of his good character.

5. The lateral ....exhibited by the new research team showed their creativity, originality, and innovation as they solved the problem.

6. Our salespeople are given financial ....for reaching their quotas.

7. The military had to................ to restore order.

8. The hedge.............. market thrived with the new players that were able to make strategic guesses backed by legitimate analysis.

9. While some people believe storing their cash in a safe will keep it secure, the value of their money will likely decline over time due to ....

10. Every computer comes with the manufacturer's ....software.

11. She is rich, but she is very................... with her money.

12. She ....as a real estate agent.

13. You should be someone that others say has high ....so that they can rely on you in times of need.

14. My manager was worried because he would be getting his .... statement today and sees how he was doing for the company.

15. The economic ....was beneficial as far as being able to purchase goods cheaper, but wages also decreased and fewer jobs were available.

16. I checked the consumer ....index to compare prices of goods and services to what their price was on the previous year.

17. Demand and prices cannot rise beyond the available purchasing................

18. My colleague tried to make some extra money in the foreign exchange markets, but he lost his investment because he didn't know anything about ....

19. The .... of payments was double checked to ensure accurate reporting was taking place because we wanted to make a presentation to the board soon.

20. Through resourcefulness and................., the pioneers survived the hardship they encountered.

21. The initial ....brought many seemingly qualified candidates into the hiring pool but unfortunately the hiring manager still needed to choose only one.

22. We're trapped in a ....circle.

23. These costs will have a huge/major ripple ....on the economy.

24. After the local resident filed a scathing complaint against the city, an .... hurriedly arrived to review the case, and begin their investigation.

25. The senior members of the firm had an open ....policy, so anyone who wanted to bring something up with them just had to walk through the door and ask.

361. PURCHASING POWER

Meaning:
Purchasing power is the money and credit available for spending and consumption of goods and services.

Example:
Demand and prices cannot rise beyond the available purchasing power.

Now look it up to understand more, and then make your sentences.

1. _____.
2. _____.
3. _____.

362. CONSUMER PRICE INDEX (CPI)

Meaning:
It is a measure of changes in the purchasing-power of a currency and the rate of inflation.

Example:
I checked the consumer price index to compare prices of goods and services to what their price was on the previous year.

Now look it up to understand more, and then make your sentences.

1. _____.
2. _____.
3. _____.

363. CURRENCY

Meaning:
Tokens used as money in a country. In addition to the metal coins and paper bank notes, modern currency also includes checks drawn on bank accounts, money orders, travelers checks, and will soon include electronic money or digital cash.

Example:
My colleague tried to make some extra money in the foreign exchange markets, but he lost his investment because he didn't know anything about currency.

Now look it up to understand more, and then make your sentences.

1. _____.
2. _____.
3. _____.

364. BALANCE OF PAYMENTS (BOP)

Meaning:
Set of accounts that record a country's international transactions, and which (because double entry bookkeeping is used) always balance out with no surplus or deficit shown on the overall basis.

Example:
The balance of payments was double checked to ensure accurate reporting was taking place because we wanted to make a presentation to the board soon.

Now look it up to understand more, and then make your sentences.

1. _____.
2. _____.
3. _____.

365. GRIT

Meaning:
Grit is mental toughness and a determined, courageous attitude.

Example:
Through resourcefulness and grit, the pioneers survived the hardship they encountered.

Now look it up to understand more, and then make your sentences.

1. _____.
2. _____.
3. _____.

Review Quiz

Fill in the blanks with the appropriate terms from the box:

> **Money, skills, consumption, independent, risks. career, job, end, resource, debt,**

Many people let .... dictate the direction their .... goes. Either they take the highest paying .... they can get now, or the one that will give them the .... they need to get the highest paying job they can get in the future. Money should certainly be a consideration, but not the only one. In our culture of...................., it's easy to forget that money is a means, not an ...., and that promotions and raises don't always lead to lasting happiness. The truly scarce ....is time, but too many people value money over time when they should be doing the reverse. Having said all that, if you are currently in............ or living paycheck to paycheck, do whatever you can to become financially .... as soon as possible. This opens up more choices in your career and your life, allowing you to focus on things other than money, think longer-term, and take more intelligent.....................

Treasure Box 25: Learning Strategy

> In order for you to gain insight into your learning and your understanding, frequent feedback is critical. You need to monitor your learning and actively evaluate your strategies and your current levels of understanding.

GETTING TRUE GRIT

Successful leaders are passionate and focus resolutely on growth. Psychologists call it grit, writes Dave Ulrich.

We learn to win. Learning **underlies** organizational agility, predicts **leadership** success, and improves individual productivity.

How do we improve our capacity to learn? Learning has two dimensions: personal energy and passion and an ability to demonstrate a growth **mind-set**. Psychologists call this virtuous combination "grit", concluding that grit is a better predictor of long-term personal, educational, and leadership success than intellect (IQ), emotion (EQ), or sociability (SQ). Here's my list of how to **enhance** grit (from research, experience, and observations.)

1. Set realistic expectations. Sometimes, we try to achieve the unachievable. Grit needs to be directed with realistic expectations.
2. Take a risk. Challenge yourself to do new things. Habits and routines are 70% to 80% of our lives, but experimenting with new routines allows us to grow. See change as opportunity not **threat**.
3. Persist in the face of **setbacks**. When trying something new, it often won't work and it is very easy to blame and rationalize. **Face** mistakes, run into them and honestly evaluate what worked and what did not work.

REVIEW QUIZ

A. MATCH EACH TERM WITH ITS APPROPRIATE MEANING

grit – to form the basis or foundation of (an idea, a process, etc.)

underlies – a particular way of thinking : a person's attitude or set of opinions about something

leadership – to increase or improve (something)

mind-set – mental toughness and courage

enhance – someone or something that could cause trouble, harm, etc.

threat – a problem that makes progress more difficult or success less likely

setbacks – the power or ability to lead other people

Face – to deal with (something bad or unpleasant) in a direct way

B. FILL IN THE SPACE WITH THE APPROPRIATE WORD FROM THE BOX

> threat, setbacks, grit, underlies, leadership,
> mind-set, enhance, face, evaluate, challenge

Successful leaders are passionate and focus resolutely on growth. Psychologists call it_____, writes Dave Ulrich.

We learn to win. Learning _____ organizational agility, predicts_____ success, and improves individual productivity.

How do we improve our capacity to learn? Learning has two dimensions: personal energy and passion and an ability to demonstrate a growth_____. Psychologists call this virtuous combination "grit", concluding that grit is a better predictor of long-term personal, educational, and leadership success than intellect (IQ), emotion (EQ), or sociability (SQ). Here's my list of how to_____ grit (from research, experience, and observations.)

1. 1. Set realistic expectations. Sometimes, we try to achieve the unachievable. Grit needs to be directed with realistic expectations.
2. Take a risk._____ yourself to do new things. Habits and routines are 70% to 80% of our lives, but experimenting with new routines allows us to grow. See change as opportunity not_____.
3. Persist in the face of_____. When trying something new, it often won't work and it is very easy to blame and rationalize._____ mistakes, run into them and honestly_____ what worked and what did not work.

Congratulations, you did it! Remember that the world is big and life is short. You can't know or do everything. In your career as in life, you need to focus, and to focus on the right things. Focus on the activities that will propel your career in the direction you want to take it and keep learning!

INDEX

A

B

C

D

K

L

M

N

O

P

338. **Pass the buck**
255. **Pick someone's brains**
191. **Per Diem**
189. **Paradigm**
166. **Parameter**
182. **Pervasive**
206. **Portfolio**
302. **Preamble**
236. **Premium**
171. **Premises**
196. **Principal**
223. **Privatization**
4. **Production**
5. **Production capacity**
6. **Product**
20. **Product liability**
342. **Proprietary**
344. **Prosper**
45. **Passive incomes**
48. **Partnership agreement**
49. **Procurement**
50. **Purchase**
361. **Purchasing power**
55. **Pro forma Statements**
64. **Productivity**
72. **Product development**
79. **Product research**
93. **Packaging**
94. **Product life cycle**
115. **Primary market**
157. **Pro forma invoice**

Q

Quick Review Quiz!

R

S

T

U

EARLIER RESOURCES

Be more proactive on your way to being fluent. Join;
englishconnect365seriesclub and connect with the
author for regular free exchange of information.